Che Guevara on Guerrilla Warfare

´CHE
GUEVARA

With an Introduction by

ON

GUERRILLA

WARFARE,

Guevara, Ernesto

Major Harries-Clichy Peterson, USMCR

FREDERICK A. PRAEGER, *Publisher*
New York

BOOKS THAT MATTER

Published in the United States of America in 1961 by
Frederick A. Praeger, Inc., Publisher
64 University Place, New York 3, N.Y.

Second printing, 1962

Library of Congress Catalog Card Number: 61-17029

The publisher expresses his appreciation to the Office of the
Assistant Chief of Staff for Intelligence, Department of the
Army, and to the Marine Corps Association for their cooperation in making their translations of *Guerrilla Warfare*
available for use in this book.

Manufactured in the United States of America

Contents

CONTENTS

vi

Introduction

The New Weapon: Communist Revolutionary Guerrilla Warfare

PREPARATIONS FOR NUCLEAR and conventional warfare are draining the world's economies. Yet, both forms of warfare are becoming increasingly less practical instruments of national policy.

Fear of reciprocal devastation has deterred nuclear warfare. Moreover, with substantial capacity for overkill on both sides, only some radically new weapon or defense, not yet revealed, or a lapse in our willpower, is likely to lift this stalemate.

Conventional warfare has been checked by Western commitments—such as NATO, CENTO, and SEATO —to react to overt aggression. Although these particular treaties have never been tested, Korea and Lebanon show that we are more or less ready and willing to resist aggression in militarily accessible areas.

But surely the Communists have not abandoned their passion to bury us. What methods will they resort to? Mr. Khrushchev already has declared economic war against us. Will this satisfy him? It is slow. It requires the painful dedication of Communism's still not abundant material and capital resources. And, it is just possible the Communists might not win that war if the West unites economically.

By contrast, guerrilla warfare has produced quick, dramatic results at low cost. It gave Communism its major ally, mainland China. It sneaked in North Vietnam, Cuba, and most of Laos. It could break out in other countries of Latin America, Africa, and Asia.

Guerrilla warfare incites no nuclear retaliation. It avoids the troops-cross-border criterion needed to activate our defensive treaties. Thus witness the inability of the Rio Pact, the United Nations, and the Organization of American States to take action with regard to Cuba. For the aggressor, guerrilla warfare has none of the heavy costs of all-out warfare. It exploits the Communists' long experience in revolutionary activities. It can be conducted in countries not contiguous to the Communist land mass. The aggressor merely finds a suitably vulnerable nation, then supplies a few catalysts:

ideology, "moral" encouragement, organizers, methods, and—at most—a minimum of war material.

Communist revolutionary guerrilla warfare is a new weapon, not to be confused with old guerrilla concepts of minor disruption of an otherwise tidy rear. First, let us clarify a few terms. Civil war is a war between two groups of the same nation. Rebellion is open, organized resistance against previously established authority. Revolution is successful rebellion. Revolt and insurrection are armed uprisings in which the outcome is quickly decided. Bandit warfare is armed fighting to support life by plunder. Partisan or orthodox guerrilla warfare is armed fighting by light troops, detached or separately established from a regular army, whose operations they support principally by harassing the common enemy, usually without seizing and defending substantial land areas. Communist revolutionary guerrilla warfare is new and different. It is a deliberate military effort inspired by international Communism, using local adherents to weaken the military, economic, and political unity of an area so that it will fall under Communist control.

This kind of aggression has now become Communism's real carving knife. Let us consider how it was developed. Actually, as surprising as it may seem, the Russian Communists have comparatively little useful experience in revolutionary guerrilla warfare. The revolt that installed the democratically minded Provisional Government in February, 1917, was virtually spontaneous and unorganized. The Communists fought this government by political intrigue and local armed detachments partly financed by Germany, and in October of the same year they stole the power for themselves.

It is true that after being overrun by the Germans in 1941–42, the Russians developed a form of partisan warfare behind the enemy lines that materially contributed to the eventual expulsion of the Germans. But the partisan motive was not revolution; it was, rather, simply the defense of the homeland against oppressive invaders, who, being totalitarians themselves, were in no position to fill the role of liberator.

After World War II, Russia added over 100 million people to Communism, not by guerrilla warfare, but simply by never relinquishing control of occupied eastern Europe and northern Japan. This was in naked —but unopposed—violation of Yalta, Potsdam, and other agreements. Where opposed, as in Yugoslavia and Greece, Russia yielded. Even today, Syria, the Kurds, the Kashmir, and islands of northern Japan present opportunities for Russia to foment guerrilla warfare, yet nothing is being done to bring about such a development. In Algeria and the Congo, Russia similarly has hesitated to involve itself openly with guerrilla warfare, despite obvious opportunities. The Russians seem to rely more on the perhaps obsolete dogma that urban workers will bring down governments by labor strife and political means alone. And, of course, Russia assists this hope with subversion and cunning diplomacy in the internal and external affairs of non-Communist nations.

It is not the Russians, but the Chinese Communists and their friends in Cuba who are best prepared to foment and exploit revolutionary guerrilla warfare in their impatience to rule the world. Foremost among Chinese masters of guerrilla warfare is Mao Tse-tung. In 1937, he recast the ancient principles of war of Sun Tse into a powerful modern doctrine in his pamphlet *Guerrilla Warfare*. Mao had just completed ten years of leadership of the 4th Red Army, formed of Communists purged from the Kuomintang. Those forces resisted five extermination campaigns by Chinese Nationalists, as well as Japanese invasions. Then, with the Japanese removed in 1945, Mao formed his ragged guerrillas into an army and, by 1949, had driven all armed opposition from the mainland, thus handing a nation of 600 million to Communism. Learning from his Korean venture that overt aggression would be opposed to some degree, Mao then successfully employed guerrilla warfare to pluck North Vietnam from

Western hands. In an obvious move for control of Southeast Asia, Mao is now extending this pattern into Laos and South Vietnam.

Although some still claim that in Cuba the revolution preceded Communism, there can be no doubt that the two are now wedded. In July, 1960, Major Ernesto (Che) Guevara published *Guerrilla Warfare,* a how-to-do-it guide for armed revolution. Speaking in Moscow in December of the same year, he declared: "Cuba stands ready to fulfill her Communist-designated goal as a model for armed revolution in Latin America."

The heart of Communist doctrine on guerrilla warfare is set forth in Mao's and Guevara's books. Both agree that the guerrilla movement grows by unifying diverse bands of irregulars who joined together in arms to resist a common enemy. The underlying motivation is not only to right wrongs inflicted by the enemy (that is to say, to destroy the existing governments), but also to build a new and "just" social order (that is to say, a Communist state). Thus, political factors are fully as important as military ones. Guerrillas are volunteers dependent upon the support of sympathetic, cooperative agrarian masses; as Mao says, they are like fish who cannot live out of water. Leadership and discipline start out with an extreme form of self-righteous puritanism governed more by individual initiative and revolutionary conscience than direct regimentation. Strategy is indirect. It begins with the need to conserve strength while adjusting to the enemy's initial superiority in men and equipment. Then, it shifts from passive survival to vicious attrition designed to weaken the enemy for the kill. Finally, guerrilla forces are formed into an army to defeat the weakened enemy by more or less conventional positional warfare.

The most hazardous and difficult step in guerrilla warfare is its initiation. Mao's rebellion first took the form of workers' uprisings; these were defeated and almost all his rebels were wiped out. He recovered only after he fled to rural areas and adopted the cause of agrarian reform. Mao never really initiated guerrilla bands at the grass-roots level. His skill lay in uniting Communist outcasts, disloyal national guards, underpaid private constabularies, and opportunistic bandits in strife-torn China. Later, an alliance with Chu Teh's army and remnants of Chinese defeated in Manchuria established a mass that Mao built into a hard Communist core, successfully overcoming skepticism and corruption. Guevara, however, one of the first co-conspirators of Castro in Mexico, landed with Castro in Cuba, and saw their tiny guerrilla band swell into a rebel army. He can speak with authority on kindling the first spark. Guevara, moreover, has no intention of repeating Mao's abortive workers' uprisings. He warns that in the cities armed revolt can all too easily be smothered when customary civil liberties are suspended or ignored, thus forcing resistance movements to act clandestinely, without arms, and against enormous dangers. He favors rural areas where guerrillas and inhabitants can cooperate closely, beyond the reach of enemy forces.

Tactics play a major role in the successful development of guerrilla warfare. The essence is hit and run. Mao says: "Withdraw when the enemy advances; harass him when he stops; strike him when he is weary; pursue him when he withdraws." He likens guerrillas to "innumerable gnats which, by biting a giant both in front and in rear, ultimately exhaust him." Guevara expresses it this way: ". . . a sudden, surprise, furious, relentless attack; then, abruptly, total passivity. The survivors think things have returned to normal, when suddenly a fresh blow lands from a new direction. An unexpected lightning blow is what counts!" As an example, Guevara cites his "minuet": The guerrillas surround the enemy, stationing small groups on all four sides. The dance begins as one side fires on the enemy, drawing him toward that side. Then another side opens fire and draws the enemy to that side. Thus, as the partners on all sides enter the dance, the enemy is immobilized, demoralized, and expends vast quantities of ammunition, while the guerrillas withdraw unharmed.

A sanctuary is an indispensable element of guerrilla warfare. Mao operated in a vast and populous country. He evaded extermination by long marches of withdrawal and by disappearing into the populace. He developed incredible skill in changing the character of his forces from guerrilla bands to organized army, back to guerrilla bands, to civilians, etc. Guevara never developed this chameleon versatility on a large scale. He began in heavily vegetated, almost inaccessible hills, and there he crippled the incumbent Cuban army, whose leaders, driven by a blind passion to eradicate all opposition immediately at any cost, saw their trap only too late: The hills that consumed them had nourished a rebel army which then emerged in the open and quickly mopped up.

As for war material, neither Mao nor Guevara received any substantial quantity from the outside. Each supplied himself principally by capturing from the enemy. Mao, being constantly subject to displacement, built up no guerrilla industry. Guevara carried on important rear-echelon industry, services, and training in his hills.

Mao paid only minor attention to urban sabotage, but Guevara saw it as a major help, which he at all times coordinated from the guerrilla headquarters in the hills.

Although both Mao and Guevara saw the implications of their experience in guerrilla warfare beyond their own countries, Guevara presses the issue with exuberant Latin confidence. He is certain that "throughout the world the pillars of colonialism are crumbling. The people are united, not by religion, race, custom, or hunger, but by common economic and social goals and by a common desire to improve their lot. Asia and Africa joined in Bandung. Now Cuba is uniting Asia and Africa with colonial America."

He brags that the Cuban revolution was recognized as an "epic triumph [revising] old dogmas about the behavior of Latin American masses and has proved the peoples' ability to free themselves from an oppressive government through guerrilla warfare." To Guevara this is opportunity knocking at the door: "Given suitable operating terrain, land hunger, enemy injustices, etc., a hard core of thirty to fifty men is, in my opinion, enough to initiate armed revolution in any Latin American country." And why be patient? "One does not necessarily have to wait for a revolutionary situation to arise; it can be created. . . . The people must be shown that social wrongs are not going to be redressed by civil means alone. And it is desirable to have the oppressor, wittingly or not, break the peace first." Finally, Guevara went one step further in his forward thinking. In his book, he includes a section on how to defend what has been won against a counterrevolution.

INTRODUCTION

Mao's methods in China have spawned a formidable offspring. Will there be more? Throughout the world, politically unstable, illiterate, poverty-stricken countries present fertile ground for Communist revolutionary warfare. To mention some: Algeria, where another billion-dollar guerrilla war is being fought; South Africa, where implacable apartheid can only lead from animosity to insurrection; Kenya, where an imaginative Communist effort could fan the Mau Mau into massive terrorism; Brazil, where peasant leagues in the backward northeast are responding to militant, collectivistic appeals; South Vietnam, where much of the strategic Mekong Delta is under the Communist Viet Cong and reports several hundred deaths monthly; Colombia, where rural violence—the typical prelude to open guerrilla warfare—holds five provinces under a state of siege; Paraguay, Nicaragua, the Dominican Republic, and Haiti where stern dictatorships have trampled representative government underfoot; Bolivia, desperately poor; Peru, where Communist infiltration has found fertile ground in the perennial drought-famined southern highlands; Panama, where pampering of U.S. Canal Zone workers and the Egyptian precedent are stirring nationalistic consciences.

For perspective, a few countries should be mentioned that are not likely prospects for an agrarian-based guerrilla war: Mexico, already "extremely left" by self-proclamation; Chile and Argentina, where a political majority of poor urban workers lured on by unrealistic social-welfare schemes has surpassed agrarian discontent as a revolutionary threat; and the Guianas, small, thinly populated territories with a colonial status that permits immediate corrective action by the ruling overseas powers with scant risk of international consequences.

Before examining what might be done against this manifold threat, let us first consider one of the very few instances, perhaps the only one, where the West turned back a fully developed Communist revolutionary guerrilla war. The country is Malaya, of approximately the same size, population, and wealth as Cuba.

Immediately after Japan surrendered, the Communists began a campaign of violence and economic sabotage designed to destroy the democratic-minded British Military Administration, and in its place erect a Communist state. The campaign progressed well, and in June, 1948, the British were forced to declare a state of emergency. Terrorism under Chin Peng, the Communist leader, mounted rapidly, reaching an average of nearly one terrorist attack each hour in 1951. Faced with a complete national collapse, the government began an all-out effort to win this guerrilla war.

First, the normal population was separated from the Communists. This was done by blocking roads and heavily guarding all cities and towns and by forcibly moving some 400,000 scattered homesteaders into fortified living compounds protected with deep barbed-wire entanglements and heavily patrolled both inside and out. For each family so moved, the government had to provide materials to build a new home and a cash resettlement allowance. Check points and identity cards were instituted to control all individual movement. Likewise, in an effort to starve out the guerrillas, all food was distributed in sealed containers, completely rationed, and strictly accounted for. In living compounds, central cooking and feeding further supported this policy. A host of concessions followed: a general amnesty, a cash reward for surrender, and a rehabilitation program including a monthly cash allowance while being de-indoctrinated and prepared to hold a useful job. Psychological appeals, backed up by fulfillment of promises, stressed protection against terrorism, job security, and generous governmental help for education, medical aid, and public works. Finally, the British gave Malaya independence and established a democratic federation.

The major factor, however, was an omnipresent, resolutely employed military force based on approximately 15,000 regular army and marine troops, 150,000 regular police, and 250,000 volunteer home guards. These forces guarded work and living areas and communications, and they attacked guerrillas vigorously, with engagements ranging from company-size combat to small hunter-killer teams composed of giant Fuji Islanders. Combat support included armored vehicles, helicopters, parachute drops, light bombers, artillery, and mortars. The military effort culminated in a thorough combing of the western mountain range and, in July, 1960, in the termination of the state of emergency —some twelve years after its beginning. The total cost has been estimated at approximately $1.2 billion: $400 million from the Malayan treasury, and $800 million from Commonwealth sources.

How strong was the guerrilla opposition? No more than 15,000 men and women, who at no time were able to get significant material help, because Malaya borders on no Communist country, and air and sea deliveries were cut off. The cost of this antiguerrilla operation averaged $80,000 for each guerrilla, a staggering sum in Asia. And the movement is not yet wiped out: Some 1,000 hard-core Communist guerrillas are still loose on the Thai border. Could the West afford this on a world-wide scale? Certainly not, for despite apparent victory in Malaya, the economic leverage clearly remains very much on the Communist side. Psychologically, too, Malaya, was not a real test of the West's ability to reverse a guerrilla movement. Communism's Malayan adherents were motivated more by fear of physical reprisal for noncooperation than by burning social convictions.

What antiguerrilla experience can the U.S. draw on? The Marines have had considerable small-wars experience prior to World War II. The lessons learned have been set forth in a Marine handbook entitled *Small Wars Manual*. The reasoning behind such employment of armed forces is very interesting to recall now.

> According to international law, as recognized by the leading nations of the world, a nation may protect, or demand protection for, its citizens and their property wherever situated. The President of the United States as the Chief Executive is, under the Constitution, primarily charged with the conduct of foreign relations, including the protection of the lives and property of United States citizens abroad, save insofar as the Constitution expressly vests a part of these functions in some other branch of the Government. (For example, the participation of the Senate in the making of treaties.) ...
>
> The use of the forces of the United States in foreign countries to protect the lives and property of American citizens resident in those countries does not necessarily constitute an act of war, and is, therefore, not equivalent to a declaration of

war. The President, as chief executive of the nation, charged with the responsibility of the lives and property of United States citizens abroad, has the authority to use the forces of the United States to secure such protection in foreign countries.

Since Marines stationed aboard naval ships throughout the world are a quick and discreet means of getting a small armed force on the scene, the precedent was established that such a Marine landing did not constitute an act of war. Functions assumed by the Marines ashore after overcoming resistance and protecting the lives and property of U.S. citizens included the disarming of natives, the training of a constabulary, and the supervision of elections. The act of intervention itself was justified as follows:

The use of force against a foreign and friendly state, or against anyone within the territories thereof, is illegal. The right of self-preservation, however, is a right which belongs to states as well as to individuals, and in the case of states it includes the protection of the state, its honor and its possessions, and lives and property of its citizens against arbitrary violence, actual or impending, whereby the state or its citizens may suffer irreparable injury.

xxii

INTRODUCTION

The key point of these Marine Corps small wars was that military and diplomatic strategy was much more closely wedded than in major wars undertaken as the last resort after all diplomatic efforts have failed. The landings in Cuba on April 17, 1961, would suggest that this technique of mutual reinforcement might now have become a lost art.

Recent Army activities have been more or less limited to providing training and advice to native forces resisting Communism, rather than taking the form of direct intervention. Since Cuba, much greater attention has been given to the several thousand elite paratroopers who make up the U.S. Army's Special Forces. Also, the Army is establishing in the Canal Zone a center to train Latin American army personnel in guerrilla fighting. The Army's new spearhead of combat, its Strategic Corps, while trained to a high degree of perfection, has not yet been employed in any foreign crisis.

Yet, the magnificent combat readiness of our Fleet Marine Force and Strategic Army Corps simply is *not* deterring Communist revolutionary guerrilla warfare. Power must be shown and used to be effective, and our expeditionary forces lack an effective employment strategy. While this condition exists, we will be conceding the initiative to the Communists as they lead us into a labyrinth of unknowns: How can we develop common agreement on the dangers posed by, and the response to be taken against, expanding international Communism? How can we develop positive means for early identification of Communist revolutionary guerrilla warfare? How can we create conditions for employing again a U.S. presence as effectively as we did in Lebanon? Must any aid we might wish to extend to anti-Communist movements be secret? If so, how do we in a democracy decide public policy for secret aid? If not, what new risks will be incurred and what reaction from Communism should we prepare for? How far might we ourselves go in using guerrilla warfare to rescue countries now under Communist control?

It is not the purpose of this foreword, nor is it possible in this limited space, to answer these questions or to suggest the needed employment strategy. Rather, this foreword is a plea to recognize clearly how Communist revolutionary guerrilla warfare delivered Cuba, and what it portends beyond. Once this is understood, an intelligent response can be made. But, until diplomatic, social, and economic means eradicate the causes that create fertile soil for Communist revolutions, it will be the military man who safeguards our national security.

Let us hypothesize a possible Communist attempt at take-over: Country X launched an economic-development program a few years ago, but lacking modern laws, fiscal discipline, trained and educated personnel, and handicapped by a one-crop economy, progress has been slow. The country, being the object of concerted Communist agitation, has succumbed to a restless minority, one hostile to any government action and convinced that only a revolution will bring about the desired social and economic progress. Anxious not to compromise a single step of its expertly planned program, the government has unwittingly permitted increasing police severity, culminating in a "Sharpsville." An insurgent leader thus is created and guerrilla bands are formed in the hills. Resistance spreads as the army, poorly trained and equipped and hardly more than a ceremonial guard, loses control of outlying areas. Finally discovering that the insurgents are aided and abetted by foreign Communists, and recognizing that progress can not be resumed until civil order is restored, the government appeals to other members of its regional defense pact, who agree to provide the assistance requested, including certain U.S. armed-forces support.

How can the U.S. military man best prepare for such a responsibility? First, the seeming hesitation of his civilian superiors to commit him to action must never deter the military man from developing new capabilities and perfecting old ones. Already our Army is exploring a radical new doctrine—how to land inside Communist-held territory and develop counterrevolutionary guerrilla warfare. We are training military advisory and assistance groups. We are perfecting new equipment for communications, helicopter movement, battlefield surveillance, and remote sensing. We are working out new tactics and techniques. One is the hunter-killer team, which will go right into the guerrilla's sanctuary and hunt down the guerrilla band day and night until it is destroyed or flushed out for the kill by larger forces. Since much of guerrilla confidence is built upon the security of a sanctuary, the mere presence of a hunter-killer team operating in its lair can completely shift guerrilla operations from offense to defense.

The hunter-killer team clearly suggests that a new emphasis—on the individual—is required in U.S. training for guerrilla fighting. Physical fitness is basic. The guerrilla fighter must be capable of sustained, fast movement on foot while carrying heavy loads. He should be able to take cliffs, rivers, and swamps in his stride. He should have a reservoir of health that will resist fatigue, wounds and disease, and support personal alertness, attention to detail, and persistent concentration. He must also know how to live off the land. Night operations will be more common than daytime exploits and will require exhaustive training. Technical skills will include communications, the handling of diverse weapons and demolitions, and medical self-aid. Wherever possible, the guerrilla fighter should be trained in the native language and learn how to organize and deal with natives.

Perhaps we will not find any simple, over-all device to reverse Communist successes in guerrilla warfare, especially when large portions of the population have become convinced that Communism will bring individual betterment. Such a struggle may well be decided engagement by engagement, with ultimate victory won by the consistently more determined and stronger side. Regimented troops trained only as interior parts of large maneuver units, devoid of personal motivation, will be at a substantial disadvantage. Therefore, the guerrilla fighter must—above all else—possess full confidence in himself, his leaders, and his cause, not so much in order to win friends and influence natives, although this is important, but to provide the motivation necessary to sustain himself as an effective initiator and decider of action in combat when away from the close commands of line warfare. Guerrilla warfare is no place for a "Korean turncoat."

The material that follows is an English-language version of Guevara's original Spanish-language edition of *Guerrilla Warfare*, first published by INRA in the summer of 1960. Fifty thousand copies have been distributed—a best-seller magnitude that is effectively radiating Guevara's message throughout Latin America. No other publication from Cuba reveals so much. Fidel Castro himself has written little since his "History Will Absolve Me" speech in 1953, and transcribed versions of his nocturnal harangues defy analysis. General Alberto Bayo, popular military adviser to the Cuban Rebel Army, has over twenty publications to his credit, including his latest *One Hundred and Fifty Questions and Answers for Guerrillas,* but his works are too personalized and disorganized to be helpful. In his book, Guevara, the mastermind, the cool thinker, generalizes on the Cuban experience and looks beyond to wholesale export.

To the English reader even Guevara may sometimes appear verbose and flowery and slow to bring out his point. But this is Guevara's strength in a part of the world where 50-per-cent illiteracy is common. Guevara's ideas (Castro's much more so) are often expressed in a nearly continuous lyrical flow of emotion that virtually overwhelms the troops. Consequently, a fairly free translation was required, taking each of Guevara's ideas as they occur and then expressing them in reasonably concise English.

The important lessons to be learned from Guevara are his motives, his method of inciting his followers, and how he uses the hills as a sanctuary, thrusting out and attacking regular forces, then withdrawing and luring them in to be devoured, all in a vicious, pulsating rhythm. I would caution the military reader never to view these guerrillas as mere harassers of the rear against whom one has to defend oneself, presumably while some other battle is going on. Guevara's techniques are intended for the take-over of politically unstable countries without full-scale army operations, until perhaps the very end, when it will be too late for us to alter the outcome.

The guerrilla challenge is not how to defend the rear, but to prevent the creation of a Communist revolutionary guerrilla movement by all means, including military, and if that fails, then to go into attack and eradicate the movement decisively and economically.

This translation was prepared by the publisher. It is based on the official U.S. Army Intelligence translation and on the condensation I wrote for the June–August, 1961, issues of the *Marine Corps Gazette*.

I hope that by reading this translation of Guevara, grasping his thinking, and recognizing the grave danger posed, all readers will be better prepared to help our country meet the challenge posed by guerrilla warfare.

HARRIES-CLICHY PETERSON
Major, U.S. Marine Corps Reserve

New York City
July, 1961

TO CAMILO

THIS MANUAL IS dedicated
to the memory of Camilo Cienfuegos. His destiny prevented him from seeing it and commenting on it. This
book is a tribute to the rebel army and to its great
captain—the greatest guerrilla leader of the revolution,
the perfect revolutionary, our friend and comrade.

Camilo fought with us in a hundred battles. The
confidant of Fidel in the most difficult moments of the
war, he was an unselfish fighter whose character and
that of his troops was strengthened by sacrifice.

I believe he would have approved this work, this
attempt to synthesize our guerrilla experiences. For
these experiences are the product of life itself, and to
them he brought the vitality of his temperament, his
intelligence, his audacity—qualities found in such pro-
fusion only rarely throughout history.

But Camilo should not be regarded as an isolated

hero whose genius permitted him to accomplish outstanding deeds. He is a very part of the people who formed him, as they form all the heroes, martyrs, and leaders of their great struggle.

I do not know whether Camilo was familiar with Danton's maxim: *"De l'audace, encore de l'audace et toujours de l'audace."* But he lived it and brought to it additional qualities vital to the guerrilla: the gift of accurate and rapid analysis of a situation and of anticipating future problems.

Although these lines, intended as a personal tribute and as the homage of an entire people to our hero, do not pretend to be a biography or a collection of legends about him, Camilo was a living legend. His ease of manner and respect for the individual were the mark of his personality, a personality that left its stamp on his every action. As Fidel has said, Camilo did not have book learning, but he had the native intelligence of the people who chose him from among thousands to lead them with audacity, tenacity, intelligence, and unequaled devotion.

Camilo practiced loyalty with religious fervor—not only personal loyalty toward Fidel who, like no one else, embodies the will of the people, but also loyalty toward the people. The people and Fidel marched forward accompanied by the devotion of this invincible guerrilla.

xxxii

TO CAMILO

Who killed him? Or rather we should ask: Who ended his physical existence? Because men such as he live on after death. Their life does not come to an end except by the will of the people.

The enemy killed him. He was killed because the enemy wanted his death. He was killed because our airplanes are not safe, because our pilots cannot acquire the necessary experience, because he was overworked and wanted to spend a few hours in Havana. His own character killed him. Camilo did not measure danger. He used it as a diversion, he toyed with it, taunted it, embraced it, and dealt with it. As a guerrilla fighter, nothing could hold him back or swerve him from a planned course of action.

He died known, admired, and loved by all the people. Had he died sooner, his story would have been the story of just another guerrilla captain. Fidel has said that there will be many Camilos, and I can add that there have been many Camilos, Camilos whose lives were ended before accomplishing the magnificent deeds that have made him part of history. Camilo and all the other Camilos—those who died too soon and those to come—are a measure of the strength of the people, they are the highest expression of what can be done by a dedicated nation fighting for its highest ideals.

We are not going to define him and imprison him in a mold. Let us leave him thus, without spelling out details of his social and economic ideology, but let us say that this war of liberation has not given us another soldier like Camilo. Dedicated revolutionary, man of the people, molder of the Cuban revolution, he never wearied or doubted. The memory of Camilo, the fighter, is evoked daily. It is he who put his unmistakable, indelible stamp on the Cuban revolution; it is he who is present in those others who died too soon and in those who are yet to come.

Che Guevara on Guerrilla Warfare

1

General Principles of
Guerrilla Fighting

1. Essence

THE ARMED VICTORY of the Cuban people over the Batista dictatorship has been recognized throughout the world as an epic triumph. It has revised old dogmas about the behavior of Latin American masses and has proved the people's ability to free themselves from an oppressive government through guerrilla warfare.

We believe that the Cuban revolution revealed three fundamental conclusions about armed revolution in the Americas:

1) Popular forces can win a war against an army.

2) One does not necessarily have to wait for a revolutionary situation to arise; it can be created.

3) In the underdeveloped countries of the Americas, rural areas are the best battlefields for revolution.

The first two conclusions refute the do-nothing attitude of those pseudo revolutionaries who procrastinate under the pretext that nothing can be done against a professional army. They also refute those who feel the need to wait until, in some perfect way, all the required objective and subjective conditions are at hand, instead of hastening to bring these conditions about through their own efforts. These undeniable truths were discussed in Cuba and are probably being discussed in Latin America now. Of course, not all the prerequisites for a revolution are going to be created solely by guerrillas. Certain minimum preconditions are needed to kindle the first spark. The people must be shown that social wrongs are not going to be redressed by civil means alone. And it is desirable to have the oppressor, wittingly or not, break the peace first.

Under these conditions, popular discontent assumes increasingly positive forms, creating a state of resistance that, provoked by the attitude of the authorities, can easily lead to an outbreak of fighting.

If a government has come to power through some form of popular vote, whether fraudulent or not, and if that government maintains at least the appearance of constitutional law, a guerrilla uprising cannot be brought about until all possible avenues of legal procedure have been exhausted.

The third conclusion is strategic, to convince those who want to center the revolution on urban masses not to overlook the tremendous role of rural people in underdeveloped America. We do not wish to underestimate the importance of armed resistance conducted by organized workers, but in the cities, armed revolt can all too easily be smothered when customary civil liberties are suspended or ignored, thus forcing resistance movements to act clandestinely, without arms, and against enormous dangers. This does not hold true in rural areas where guerrillas and inhabitants cooperate closely, beyond the reach of oppressor forces.

We place the above-mentioned three conclusions at the head of this work despite the detailed analysis to follow, for they constitute the basic contribution of the Cuban experience.

Guerrilla warfare, the basis of the people's fight for liberation, has many different characteristics and facets. It is obvious—and all who have written about it concur —that war is subject to certain strategic laws, and those who violate these laws will be defeated. Guerrilla warfare, a phase of general warfare, must be governed by all these laws; but in addition it has its own laws, and this unique set of rules must be followed if it is to succeed. Of course, different geographic and social factors in individual countries may call for different methods and forms of guerrilla warfare, but the basic laws apply to all guerrilla campaigns.

It is our task here to present these basic considerations, to develop a theory, to define and draw conclusions from our experience for the benefit of other peoples fighting for freedom.

Who are the combatants in guerrilla warfare? On one side, we have the oppressive oligarchy with its agent, the professional army, well armed and disciplined and frequently the recipient of foreign aid. Allied with the army are pampered bureaucracies. On the other side stand the people of the nation or region concerned. Guerrilla warfare is a fight of the masses, with the guerrilla band as the armed nucleus. The bands need not be considered inferior to the opposing army. Rather, the contrary is true: One resorts to guerrilla warfare when oppressed by superior numbers and arms. For the individual guerrilla warrior, then, wholehearted help from the local population is the basis on which to start. Popular support is indispensable. Let us consider the example of robber bands that roam a certain region. They possess all the characteristics of a guerrilla band

—homogeneity, respect for their leader, bravery, familiarity with the terrain, and frequently even thorough understanding of tactics. They lack only one thing: the support of the people. And inevitably, these bands are caught and wiped out by police forces.

Why does the guerrilla fight? He is a social reformer. He takes up arms in response to widespread popular protest against an oppressor, impetuously hurling himself with all his might against anything that symbolizes the established order. More on this later.

When we analyze the tactics of guerrilla warfare, we see that the guerrilla must possess a highly developed knowledge of the terrain on which he operates, avenues of access and escape, possibilities for rapid maneuver, popular support, and hiding places. All this favors rural areas. Moreover, here the guerrilla can represent the desires of the great mass of poor farmers to possess their own land, animals, and all that makes up their life from cradle to grave. In other words, the guerrilla is—above all else—an agrarian revolutionary. So, for an up-to-date understanding of guerrilla warfare, what we are interested in is an armed group that fights the existing government, whether colonial or not, that acts on its own initiative, is rural in character, and economically is based on the desire to hold land. Mao Tsetung's China began as workers' uprisings that were defeated and almost wiped out. It recovered only when

7

it took seat in rural areas and adopted the cause of agrarian reform. Ho Chi-minh's victory in Indochina was based on poor rice farmers oppressed by French colonists. In Algeria, Arab nationalism is bolstered by oppressive conditions of sharecropping imposed by French colonists. In Puerto Rico, special conditions so far have prevented a guerrilla outbreak, but nationalism is arising because the poor farmers want their land back from the Yankee invader. This same craving drove the farmers of Eastern Cuba to fight, ever since Batista first came to power thirty years ago, for the right to hold land.

This type of hostility feeds on itself, and eventually transforms guerrilla warfare into positional warfare as the strength and number of fighting units increase. The possibility for such transformation is as great as the chance to destroy the enemy whenever encountered. Therefore, never undertake any fight that cannot be won.

There is a saying: "The guerrilla is the maverick of war." He practices deception, treachery, surprise, and night operations. Thus, circumstances and the will to win often oblige him to forget romantic and sportsmanlike concepts. Military strategy and tactics represent the way the group conceives its objectives of taking full advantage of the enemy's weak points. Individual combat is much the same in guerrilla warfare as at the squad level in conventional warfare. When trickery does not work, it's only because the enemy is alert and cannot be caught off guard. However, because the guerrilla band commands itself and because the enemy cannot forever guard all areas, suprise is always possible. It is the guerrilla's duty to exploit it!

Some disparaging people call this "hit and run." That is exactly what it is! Hit and run, wait, stalk the enemy, hit him again and run, do it all again and again, giving no rest to the enemy. Perhaps this smacks of not facing up to the enemy. Nevertheless, it serves the goal of guerrilla warfare: to conquer and destroy the enemy.

It is obvious that guerrilla warfare is a preliminary step, unable to win a war all by itself. What happens is that the guerrilla army swells in size until it becomes a regular army. Only then will it be ready to deliver a knock-out blow.

Just as a division commander no longer has to sacrifice himself out front leading his troops, the guerrillas —each one his own commander—do not have to sacrifice themselves in battle. A guerrilla is willing to give his life to realize an ideal, not merely to defend it.

Thus, the essence of guerrilla warfare is the miracle by which a small nucleus of men—looking beyond their immediate tactical objective—becomes the vanguard of a mass movement, achieving its ideals, establishing a new society, ending the ways of the old, and winning social justice. Considered in this light, guerrilla warfare takes on a true greatness, a sense of destiny, without the need for further rhetoric. Likewise, an unfaltering will to fight and persistence against immense obstacles are the greatness of the guerrilla.

2. *Strategy*

In guerrilla terminology, strategy means the analysis of the objectives we wish to attain.

First, determine how the enemy will operate, his manpower, mobility, popular support, weapons, and leadership. Then, plan a strategy to best confront these factors, always keeping in mind that the final objective is to destroy the enemy army.

Once this study is made, the objectives evaluated and analyzed, it is necessary to proceed with planning of measures for attainment of the final objective. These plans will have to be made in advance, but they will be changed as needed during the fighting and adapted to any unforeseen circumstances that may arise.

In the case of weapons, consider how they are to be used, the realistic value of such items as tanks and airplanes in guerrilla warfare, the enemy's small arms, ammunition, his customs, etc. Keep in mind that the guerrilla's most important source of supply is the enemy himself. So, if there is a choice, use the same type of weapons, because the greatest danger lies in running out of ammunition—an item that must be captured from the enemy.

At the start, take special pains that no guerrilla needlessly gets himself killed. Then, as his new life becomes an everyday affair, he will instinctively duck and throw off scent any hostile forces trying to hunt him down. He takes up positions whose inaccessibility keeps the enemy away, or he amasses forces that discourage enemy attack. Now, the guerrilla can begin a campaign of attrition, first in the places nearest antiguerrilla activity, then deep into the enemy's territory to attack his communications, harass his bases, and lash out in every conceivable way.

The guerrilla must hammer away constantly. The enemy soldier caught in this operation is not allowed to sleep, his posts are attacked and systematically liquidated. Throughout the day in woods and crags, and throughout the night in open country, the enemy is made to feel that he is inside hostile jaws.

To put the enemy in such a state of mind, the guerrilla must have absolute cooperation from the people living in the area and an intimate knowledge of the terrain. This requires that, simultaneously with terrain studies, he conduct an intensive campaign on the purpose of the revolution, stressing the unquestionable truth that those who hold out against the people are going to lose. Anyone who does not feel this truth cannot be a guerrilla.

The campaign begins with care, asking each person spoken to not to reveal anything he has seen or heard. Next, the guerrilla seeks out persons of obvious loyalty to the revolution for use as contacts, carriers of weapons and supplies, and guides. Then, he goes to the urban masses to bring about a general strike.

Such a strike is crucial, but to achieve it requires a chain of events that seldom takes place spontaneously. The necessary conditions must be created. This is done by explaining the purposes of the revolution and arranging incidents that display the people's power.

The guerrilla employs sabotage to paralyze entire armies, stop industry, leave people without work, light, water, communications, or courage to venture upon the street. If all of this is carried off, the morale of the enemy and his front-line troops will crumble, leaving him ripe for plucking.

All of this assumes an increase in the size of the territory dominated by guerrillas and hence deserves a word of caution: Do not overextend the base of operations. Build it up carefully by indoctrinating local residents, neutralizing counterrevolutionaries, and perfecting defensive installations such as trenches, mines, and interior communications. Only when the guerrilla band reaches a respectable force in arms and numbers are new columns formed.

After a while, the territory occupied by guerrilla columns becomes too small for good protection and, in their advance toward the enemy's stronghold, the columns will come up against powerful opposition. At this moment, the columns unite into a compact fighting front and undertake a war of positions. Even so, the old guerrilla army cannot cut itself off from its bases. Hence, it forms new guerrilla bands behind the enemy to deliver still other hostile blows. Thus, the attack carries itself to the city, defeats reinforcements, inflames the whole country, and attains its ultimate objective: victory.

3. *Tactics*

Tactics is the practical means used to achieve strategic objectives. Compared to end objectives, tactics generally are much more flexible. While some tactical objectives do not change, others will vary considerably, adjusting themselves to fit each moment of battle.

The guerrilla relies on mobility. This permits him quickly to flee the area of action whenever necessary,

Guerrillas surround enemy column and open fire from one flank.

Enemy returns fire and sends out counterattack force. Guerrillas shift fire to second flank, withdraw from first flank.

Guerrillas shift fire to rear, withdraw on flanks.

Guerrillas shift fire to front. Withdraw rear attack.

Enemy column is pulled apart suffering heavy losses. Guerrillas withdraw before risking losses.

THE "MINUET"

constantly to shift his front, to evade encirclement (a most dangerous situation for the guerrilla), and even to counterencircle the enemy.

Speaking of counterencirclement, several examples come to mind: Small groups of guerrillas apparently are surrounded by the enemy, then all of a sudden the enemy himself is surrounded by larger forces. Or, the enemy is lured out by an impregnably located decoy, then surrounded and annihilated and his supplies seized. Another maneuver, frequently used to wear down a larger-size enemy force, is called the "minuet." The guerrillas surround the enemy, an advancing column for example, on all four sides. Five or six guerrillas are stationed on each side, sufficiently spread out to avoid their own encirclement. The dance begins as one side fires on the enemy, who naturally moves toward that side. The guerrillas on that side move back, without breaking visual contact, and succeed in drawing the enemy out. Then another guerrilla side begins firing and draws out the enemy to a different side. Thus, as the partners on all sides participate in the dance, the enemy column is rendered immobile, expends vast quantities of ammunition, and loses morale, while the guerrillas remain unharmed.

The same maneuvers can be employed at night, but at closer range and with greater aggressiveness to overcome the inherent difficulties of a night encirclement.

In general, night operations are important for the guerrilla, for they enable him to advance to lines of departure or otherwise move around in unfamiliar areas with less danger of being reported.

The guerrilla's numerical inferiority makes it necessary always to attack by surprise, permitting him to inflict disproportionate losses upon the enemy. Such an advantage is indispensable, because with equal casualties on both sides, the numerically inferior guerrilla band would be wiped out much sooner than the more numerous enemy

Arms and ammunition are extremely precious items on the battlefield. Never leave a dead guerrilla behind without first rcovering his gear. Similarly, take great care in conserving ammunition. In a fire fight, one can always distinguish the regular, with his shotgun shooting, from the guerrilla taking isolated well-aimed shots.

Once, one of our heroes, now dead, had to use his machine gun for almost five minutes, burst after burst, to prevent the advance of enemy soldiers. This caused considerable confusion in our forces, because the rhythm of fire led them to believe that this key position had fallen to the enemy. This was one of the first occasions when the importance of the point defended made it necessary to suspend the rule of conserving fire.

Another characteristic of the individual guerrilla is

his initiative. In contrast to the rigidity of classical warfare, the guerrilla invents his own tactics for each moment of battle and constantly surprises his enemy.

A major responsibility of guerrilla leaders is the proper choice of the time and place to defend a position to the end. If a first-class terrain study finds an impregnable position in the path of the enemy's advance, he can be stopped cold by just a few guerrillas.

The way a guerrilla army attacks also is different: a sudden, surprise, furious, relentless attack; then, abruptly, total passivity. The survivors think things have returned to normal, when suddenly a fresh blow lands from a new direction. An unexpected lightning blow is what counts!

Sabotage is an important revolutionary means, but it should be differentiated from terrorism. Indiscriminate terrorism against groups of ordinary people is inefficient and can provoke massive retaliation. However, terrorism to repay the cruelty of a key individual in the oppressor hierarchy is justifiable. But it must never be used to eliminate unimportant individuals whose death would accomplish nothing but invite retaliation. There remains another point regarding terrorism, a controversial one. Many feel that once terrorism is used and the oppressor angered, sympathetic communication with the masses will be more difficult. That is true as far as it goes. But, often the oppressor's grip is so tight that nothing can be done anyway, except by force of arms. It comes down to a calculated risk.

If well conducted, sabotage is an effective weapon. But do not knock out industries and put people needlessly out of work without helping to achieve the revolution's goals. For example, stopping a soft-drink factory will not paralyze a whole sector of the oppressor's economy; blowing up an electric plant will. We will have more to say on sabotage later.

Aviation is a favorite weapon of the enemy, but it really contributes nothing during the preliminary phases when the guerrillas are scattered in the hills. Aviation is effective in the systematic destruction of organized, visible defenses or of troops on the march in open country in daytime.

One of the enemy's weakest points is highway and rail transport. It is practically impossible to guard every inch of a highway or railroad. The route and/or transport passing over it can easily be blown up.

Explosives may be obtained through various sources: They can be purchased, extracted from unexploded enemy shells or bombs, or manufactured clandestinely. In Cuba we made our own gunpowder and invented various tricky devices to set it off. A highway ambush —mining the truck and shooting the survivors—made the most efficient use of our munitions: The enemy was surprised, had no time to return fire, and could not flee. These various techniques can be perfected. In Algeria, for example, remote-control mines are being used against the French colonial forces—i.e., mines exploded from afar by electronic devices. The mining of roads and the annihilation of men yields valuable equipment and weapons. The surprised enemy does not have time to use his ammunition, which thus falls to the guerrillas.

Of course the enemy will react and, instead of dispatching single vehicles, will send through armed convoys. The answer is good selection for an ambush site, breaking up the column, and concentrating fire. Also, guard escape and reinforcement routes, know the local population and get them to help out on supplies and transport, roadblocking, and care of wounded. If all these precautions are followed, the effect on enemy communication will pay rich dividends.

An important aspect of guerrilla tactics is the treatment accorded the population of the region, including the enemy. Be relentless in the attack and toward traitors, but merciful toward those who fought only because they were forced to by the oppressor. If there are no protected operating bases, do not take prisoners; let them go free and give whatever aid you can to the wounded. In your conduct toward the civilian population, show great respect and demonstrate the guerrillas' moral superiority. Do not execute anyone without a hearing unless the situation permits no other alternative.

4. *Fighting in Favorable Terrain*

Guerrilla warfare will not always be waged in favorable terrain. But the same basic principles and tactics will apply even when the guerrilla band is located in areas of difficult and intricate access, such as jagged mountains or swamps. Contact with the enemy is important. If the region is completely inaccessible to an organized army, the guerrillas should advance to areas where they can engage the enemy in combat.

With a naturally well-protected refuge, guerrillas can come out to fight in the day as well as night, they are less restrained by enemy land and air observation, they can wage battle with fewer men and for longer duration, and hostile reinforcements can be held off.

Needless to say, the guerrilla must constantly guard all avenues of approach, but this should not deter him from aggressive action. He can come ever closer to the enemy, harass him, fight him more directly and for longer stretches—always subject to the existing conditions, such as quantity of available equipment, for example.

The disadvantage of such warfare is the difficulty

of capturing in a single action a large quantity of arms and ammunition. This is more or less compensated, however, by the relative ease of establishing, free from enemy interference, service activities such as hospitals, training centers, supply dumps, propaganda mills, etc. Moreover, the entire guerrilla force can be better integrated between fighters and service forces, trainees and veterans, etc.

The number of individuals in a guerrilla band is quite flexible. It depends on the terrain, supply facilities, mass flights of oppressed people from other areas, available arms, organizational needs, etc. There is nothing wrong with staying put for a while and accumulating more and more fighters.

The band's radius of action usually is five or six hours, determined by the number of hours of darkness available to leave protected ground, reach the point of action, and return.

Preferred weapons are those of long range and low ammunition-expenditure rates, supported by some automatic or semiautomatic weapons. One of the best small arms is the M-1—the Garand. However, it must be used only by experienced people, for it can waste much ammunition. Medium-weight weapons, such as tripod-mounted machine guns, offer a better margin of safety in favorable terrain, but only as a weapon of containment, not assault.

21

A good set of weapons for a band of twenty-five men would be ten to fifteen single-shot rifles and approximately ten automatic weapons, such as the Garand, sub-machine guns, the Browning automatic rifle, the modern Belgian FAL, or the U.S. M-14. Heavy arms, aviation, cannons, and tanks have little utility value in the type of terrain that is favorable for guerrilla warfare.

Supplying guerrilla strongholds in such terrain is difficult not only because of transport, but also because of local scarcity. It is a constant struggle and it is therefore best to build up some reserves against contingencies. For transport, use mules and, for the last stretch, man haul. Figure a sustained 55-pound load per man. For exterior communication, use a chain of trustworthy people to store supplies and provide hiding places when needed. Internal lines of communication, whose extent will depend on the strength of the guerrilla force, must also be set up. During the Cuban War, the guerrilla forces in some areas of operation set up an extensive telephone system, built roads, and organized a well-functioning messenger system. Some other methods not used in the Cuban campaign also come to mind, such as smoke signals, light signals relayed with mirrors, and homing pigeons.

It is imperative that the guerrilla forces keep their weapons in good condition, conserve equipment and supplies, and, most important, be equipped with good footwear. Therefore, all efforts should be directed toward establishing industrial workshops for the repair and, eventually, the manufacture of shoes, as well as for the manufacture of gunpowder—a fairly simple matter, yet important. Mine fields constitute a serious danger for the enemy. Hundreds of men can be killed by a single ganged explosion.

5. *Fighting in Unfavorable Terrain*

To wage guerrilla warfare in more or less open country, all the regular principles have to be followed with even more skill and intensity. The maximum possible mobility is required. Strike lightning-swift blows, preferably at night. Withdraw in a different direction.

During the night a man can march 20 to 25 miles. This can be stretched into the early hours of daybreak if the area is not closely guarded and one can risk being seen by the local inhabitants. Introduce variety in the routine, so as not to invite prearranged ambush.

Since shock, not sustained attack, is the key to fighting in open country, emphasize automatic weapons. At night, especially, it is not marksmanship, but concentration of fire at a short distance that will annihilate the enemy.

Also important is the mining of roads and blowing up of bridges. Aggressiveness will be vented in the frequency and violence of attacks rather than their duration. For example, a shotgun loaded with buckshot is an excellent weapon to greet passing trucks and buses carrying troops. This is not a guerrilla secret. Such weapons have been used in many major wars. U.S. platoons used shotguns fitted with bayonets to attack machine-gun nests.

Staying supplied with munitions to continue fighting is always a touchy problem for guerrillas. The guerrilla never attacks the enemy—even if it seems likely that he can annihilate him—if it means he will expend all his ammunition and cannot immediately resupply himself. In guerrilla warfare, ammunition must remain a constant concern. Therefore, except in areas where ammunition can be obtained, the arms used by guerrillas should match those of the enemy.

A good number of men for a guerrilla band fighting in open country is ten or fifteen at the most. This number provides good mutual support, presents a formidable front when fires are massed, yet can readily scatter and hide itself when necessary, and the danger of detection when encamped is not too great. Bear in mind that the march rate of a guerrilla force is determined by its slowest member. It is more difficult to establish uniform marching speeds among forces numbering twenty, thirty, or forty men than among those numbering ten. The plains guerrilla must be a swift runner, and it is in open country that hit-and-run tactics reach their fullest expression.

Lacking good cover and concealment, and therefore easily surrounded, the plains guerrilla trusts no one whose loyalty is not proved. Enemy retaliation is so brutal, not only against men, but also against women and children, that only the very strongest will be able to withhold information about the location and operation of the guerrilla band. This could produce an encirclement of most disagreeable, although not necessarily fatal, consequences.

For major attacks, guerrillas can be massed, but immediately thereafter they must withdraw in small, widely dispersed groups. Virtual armies can be organized under a single command without actually merging the various groups. The secret is to be sure to elect the right chief for each band, one who, ideologically and personally, will work well with the maximum leader of the zone.

Because of its ease of transport and operation, the bazooka is a very useful weapon, replacing antitank rifle grenades against armored vehicles, troop-carrying trucks, or pillboxes. Make each shot count, for on the march a man can carry a maximum of only three rockets.

If heavy weapons are captured, it would be natural to try to use them. Heavy machine guns can be readily used, but one must resign oneself to eventually abandoning them in order not to lose the mobility required for fighting in open country. In any other case, however, the loss of weapons would be inexcusable.

Supply in open country is much easier because the inhabitants are more numerous. Hammocks, blankets, waterproof wrapping, mosquito netting, shoes, medicine, and food can be readily obtained through loyal civilians and ordinary stores. If the group is small, it will not be too difficult to get meals.

Communications will be fairly easy with respect to contacting and moving about greater numbers of men. But it will be much harder to relay safely a message to a distant point, because the security risk multiplies with the number of handlers. Oral messages, after being repeated too often, get distorted; therefore it is better to use written messages in code.

In view of the above-mentioned reasons, industrial activities on the part of guerrillas, such as the manufacture of shoe soles or weapons, will not be possible. At best, the situation will permit the establishment of small, well-concealed workshops for making cartridges, mines, and other detonating devices—whatever seems most vital at a given moment. On the other hand, it may be possible to utilize the workshops of friendly local inhabitants.

When all factors are considered, two conclusions emerge: First, what is favorable for civilian life usually is not favorable for guerrilla warfare. The more facilities exist to ease the life of the civilian population, the more difficult the life of the guerrilla becomes. Well-developed means of communication, urban centers, large concentrations of people, etc.—all these factors militate against the guerrilla. Second, because of the serious consequences of betrayal in open country, great efforts must be made to proselytize the inhabitants. Any defection must be dealt with summarily. There can be no enemies in vital positions within the area of operation.

6. *Fighting in Built-up Areas*

If it should happen that the battle is pursued right up to the outskirts of a city and seems to lodge there with some permanency, special procedures will be required.

But first let it be stated that a guerrilla band never arises by itself in a suburban area. Such a band will form only when a favorable environment has been created by others, and the band will always be under direct orders of superiors situated outside. Accordingly, the mission of this band will not be to act independently, but to follow preconceived strategic plans. In other words, a suburban band will not be able to choose between knocking down telephone poles or ambushing patrolling soldiers; it will do exactly as told. If its job is to cut telephone poles, electric cableways, sewerage lines, water conduits, or railways, it will confine itself to do just these things, and do them to perfection.

Such a band should not number more than four or five men. This is important because the suburban guerrilla is working in exceptionally unfavorable terrain, where the risks and consequences of exposure are tremendous. There is only little distance between the guerrilla's point of action and his refuge, so night action must predominate. He does not emerge into the open until the insurgents besiege the city.

Essential qualities of the suburban guerrilla are discipline, probably to a degree unexcelled by any other, and discretion. He does not count on more than two or three friendly houses where he can get fed, since encirclement inside a house would be fatal. His only armament is a small, easily concealed personal weapon that will not hamper him while running. His action is limited to surprising one or two enemy troops or carrying out sabotage on order.

ON GUERRILLA WARFARE

For sabotage he needs good saws, lots of dynamite, picks and shovels, railway crowbars—all items that can be easily hidden, yet easily gotten to when needed.

If there is more than one guerrilla band, all will operate under a single chief, who will issue orders through civilian contacts of proved loyalty. Sometimes a guerrilla can continue in his civilian work, but this is very difficult. Usually the suburban guerrillas operate beyond the law in military fashion and with all the unfavorable aspects cited.

The importance of suburban fighting has not been fully appreciated. When done effectively and extended over a wide area, it completely paralyzes the everyday life of the sector. The population becomes restless, anguished, almost anxious for the development of violence, in order to bring the matter to an end. If, at the very start of the war, specialists are organized for suburban guerrilla work, quicker action can be obtained, more lives spared, and the nation's valuable time saved.

2

The Guerrilla Band

1. *The Individual Guerrilla: A Social Reformer*

WE SAID THE guerrilla is a crusader for the people's freedom who, after exhausting peaceful means, resorts to armed rebellion. He aims directly at destroying an unjust social order and indirectly at replacing it with something new. We have emphasized how conditions in the economically underdeveloped countries of the world, particularly the Americas, favor beginning the fight in rural areas and aiming at changing the ownership of farm lands. Hence, the guerrilla makes "agrarian reform" his banner. Initially, this platform may fail to outline all its aspirations and scope. It may simply recognize the peasant's yearning for the land he cultivates or wants to cultivate. The conditions under which agrarian reform can be realized depend upon those that existed before the beginning of the struggle and upon its social impact. To attain the stature of a true crusader, the guerrilla must display impeccable moral conduct and strict self-control. He must be an ascetic. At first, he will not stress social reform, acting more as a big brother to the poor farmer in matters of technology, economics, morals, and culture. He does not steal; if he cannot pay, he leaves IOU's. He bothers the rich as little as possible.

Then, little by little, the issues sharpen, people are forced to take sides, and conflict breaks out. At this point, the guerrilla emerges as the people's standard-bearer, justly punishing any betrayal of the cause, taking from the rich, and giving to the poor. If the former owner wants payment, he gives him bonds. These "bonds of hope" bind old and new owner to a common hope for the success of the cause. Whenever there is a particularly juicy plum to be handed out, he tries to set it up as a people's collective, if the popular mentality is ready for this.

The guerrilla provides ideology for social reform by personal example—by his ideas, his plans, and lessons from experience. He stresses the force of arms and spiritual dedication. Guerrilla leaders are not men bowed down by daily farm labor. They are men who see the need for agrarian social reform and team up with the people for this goal. First, they personally set the example of armed rebellion. Then, the people get the idea and carry it forward with practical improvements, thus snowballing it into nationwide rebellion.

2. The Guerrilla as a Combatant

The individual guerrilla warrior must have the right physical, mental, and moral attributes to do his job. He should come from the area in which he will fight. This will give him personal contacts, terrain knowledge, local acclimatization, and a sense of fighting for his own area.

Working mostly at night, the guerrilla first finds concealment. When ready, he comes out via a safe route to strike the enemy by surprise, destroying, killing, and sowing panic. But the guerrilla spares the defenseless, leaves enemy dead alone, and aids those enemy wounded whose previous conduct does not warrant death. Unless he has an impregnable hide-out, the guerrilla does not take prisoners because, if they escaped, they could tip off the enemy to the location of the band's lair. Except for the worst enemy criminals, the guerrilla disarms his prisoners, gives them a scolding, and then lets them go.

The guerrilla must constantly guard against encirclement. Not only is it physically disastrous, but it makes other guerrillas skeptical of being able to conduct casualty-free hit-and-run operations.

A guerrilla must be audacious and optimistic, even amidst unfavorable conditions and circumstances. He must be adaptable, imaginative, and inventive.

A guerrilla never abandons a wounded comrade to enemy mercy. Cost what it may, guerrilla wounded are carried off to a safe spot.

A guerrilla fighter must be discreet. He never reveals what he has heard, even to his fellow fighters, for the enemy will always try to introduce spies into the guerrilla ranks.

The guerrilla is physically tough and capable of enduring extremes, not only in deprivation of food, water, clothing, and shelter, but also in bearing sickness and wounds without medical care, for leaving the battle zone brings with it the risk of capture and death.

All these conditions presuppose an iron constitution, the strength to survive illness and adversity, the ability to live like a harassed animal. The guerrilla must become a part of the very soil on which he fights.

We may also ask ourselves whether a guerrilla army must reflect a specific social pattern. It has already been said that the social composition must reflect that of the area in which the guerrilla force operates. In other words, it must have a peasant nucleus. Although the peasant makes the best soldier, other parts of the population should not be excluded from fighting for a just cause. Besides, there always are personal exceptions.

What is the best age for a guerrilla? It depends on a person's background. Generally, sixteen to forty years is satisfactory when the band lacks a fixed base, but twenty-five- to thirty-five-year-old men are to be preferred. One of the heroes of the Cuban war, Major Crescencio Perez, joined our forces at the age of sixty-five and became one of our best soldiers. We believe that, aside from special circumstances, those below sixteen years of age should not be permitted to join in the fight. As a rule, these youngsters, almost children, lack the required maturity to withstand the hardships and suffering to which they would be subjected, whereas older men who are ready to leave their homes and children—their entire world—must have given thought to their responsibilities. Of course, there have been extraordinary fighters even among children. But for every one of these, there were many whose conduct placed a heavy burden on the rebel army during much of the fighting.

The guerrilla fighter is a soldier who, like a snail, carries his home upon his shoulders, and therefore his pack must contain the smallest quantity of items of the greatest possible utility. He must carry only essential articles and guard them against loss.

Similarly, his arms are also only those he can carry with him. It is very difficult to get new supplies, especially ammunition. He must protect his arms against moisture, inspect them regularly, keep his rifle clean, well oiled, and the bore shining. The chief of each group must mete out punishment to those who do not abide by these rules.

Men so dedicated must have an ideal, one that is plain and simple and worth dying for. The right to have their own land and the enjoyment of fair social treatment motivate farm laborers. For industrial workers, it is having a job, a decent wage, and social justice. For students and professional workers, the ideal is more abstract, such as freedom.

Living conditions in the field are rough. The guerrilla normally is on the march, eating when he can—sometimes he has a fabulous feast, other times he experiences two or three days of starvation, without letting up on his regular tasks. He lives under the open skies, sleeping in a hammock, his back-pack, rifle, and ammunition— his most precious possessions—protected by a nylon rain cloth. He goes on and on, hunted and being hunted, suffering cold and heat, sweating and drying out, with-

35

out time for personal cleanliness. In Cuba, it was literally a stinking life. Even individual hammocks could be identified by their smell. Security is paramount: no footprints, quickly broken encampments, 10 to 20 per cent of the personnel awake and on watch while the others sleep, etc. The guerrilla soon learns a number of tricks to make his food more palatable, diversified, and to prepare it more speedily. He learns to live on tubers, grain, and an occasional piece of meat.

Combat comes as welcome relief from this drudgery and leaves the band with freshened spirits. It begins at the right moment, upon discovering an enemy encampment sufficiently weak to be wiped out, or upon entry of a hostile column into guerrilla territory. The two cases are different.

Even though surrounded, a well-dug-in enemy with powerful weapons is poor prey. Therefore, the guerrillas make their main effort against rescue columns. Busily moving, ignorant of the terrain, apprehensive of everything, and without natural defensive protection, a rescue column is easy prey. It can be taken by surprise at two or three points, sliced in pieces, and—if not completely annihilated—left without hope of catching the withdrawing attacker.

If very greatly outnumbered by the enemy column, guerrillas concentrate on the enemy's leading elements.

Even if no important skirmishes are won, the main body again and again will see their comrades up front come back on stretchers. This will weaken enemy morale and make it difficult to man the point.

The ease with which the guerrilla carries out his tasks and adjusts to his environment depends upon his equipment. For us in Cuba, essential gear included hammock, nylon rain cloth, blanket, jacket, pants, shirt, shoes, canvas back-pack, and food such as butter or oil, canned goods, preserved fish, condensed or powdered milk, sugar, and salt. The hammock was the key to a good night's sleep. String it between two trees under the nylon rain cloth, which can be draped over a single line between the same trees and held out by four corner lines to the earth. A blanket is indispensable, for it gets very cold in the mountains. Dress consists of work shirt and work trousers, matching or not. Shoes must be sturdy. They are among the most important articles of clothing. If at all possible, each soldier should have an extra pair.

Nonessentials included: mess plate, spoon, all-purpose knife, rifle oil, cleaning rod and patches, a good cartridge belt that will not lose ammunition, canteen, medical kit, tobacco, matches, and soap. Also useful were: compass, extra nylon rain cloth, change of clothes, pants, underwear, towel, toothbrush and paste, reading books (such as biographies of heroes, history, and economic geography), machete, bottle of gasoline or piece of resinous wood to ignite damp firewood, notebook, pen or pencil, piece of rope, and sewing kit.

The guerrilla who carries this gear will have a solid house on his back, heavy but sufficient to assure him a reasonably comfortable life during the hard toil of the campaign.

3. Guerrilla Organization

Do not fix guerrilla organization. Tailor it to your needs. In Cuba, our basic unit was the squad, headed by a lieutenant with eight to twelve men. Usually, four squads made up a platoon, and four platoons a column. We had thirty to forty men in a platoon, headed by a captain. Our column had 100 to 150 men, headed by a major. We never called anyone a corporal or sergeant, because these were ranks held under the former dictatorial regime. Every platoon and squad must appoint qualified alternate commanders to take over in case the commanders are killed.

Now, let us discuss command policies in some of the more common areas. Food was distributed share and share alike. This is important, not only because the distribution of food is the one regular daily event, but

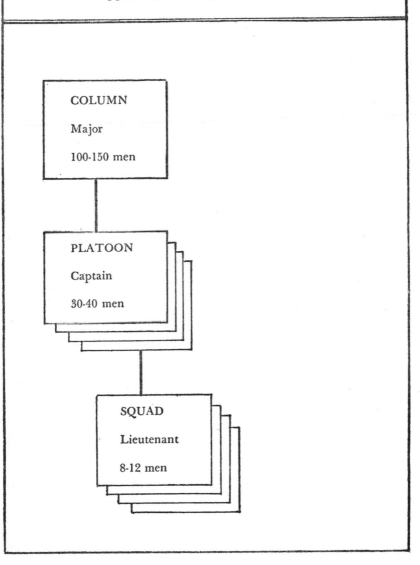

CUBAN GUERRILLA ORGANIZATION

Showing units, CO's rank, and approximate strength

COLUMN

Major

100-150 men

PLATOON

Captain

30-40 men

SQUAD

Lieutenant

8-12 men

also because the soldiers are sensitive to fancied injustices and displays of favoritism. Clothing was distributed by need, seniority, and individual merit; candy and tobacco as a common minimum, plus extras for hardship assignments. Distribution was made by specially appointed persons, preferably headquarters personnel. In general, headquarters fulfills the very important administrative duty of coordination, and the most intelligent officers should be assigned there. Its soldiers should be the most dedicated, for as a rule the demands made on them will be greater than those made on the rest of the troops. However, they are not to receive any special treatment in regard to food.

The work of carrying unit supplies was shared equally if all troops were armed. Otherwise, the unarmed usually were organized as porters. Encampments were made on high ground dominating a wide area by day and hard to reach by night. Defenses were constantly improved and, if the stay was for more than a few days, dug-outs with overhead protection against mortar fire were constructed. Camp discipline was controlled by a special committee chosen from the most meritorious revolutionaries. Discipline is a must. The soldiers should retire and arise at fixed hours. They should not be permitted to idle away their time at games. Alcohol is out. No fires that could reveal the location of the guerrilla troops are to be built.

On the march, maintain strict silence. Transmit orders by arm and hand signals or pass them in whispers. Have leading elements precede the main body by 100 to 200 meters. Scout out flanks and have rear elements erase signs of passage. Strictly adhere to march order, regardless of the number of platoons in the column. No lights are to be lit during night marches. Light is the night enemy of the guerrilla.

Before launching an attack, drop packs and make a reliable reconnaissance. If the attack is made against a fortified position only to lure in reinforcements to be ambushed, the commander must be quickly and constantly informed of all developments to avoid counter-encirclement. At night, with enough courage, you probably could assault and wipe out the same position without too much risk.

In the encirclement, dig in every time you squeeze toward the enemy, try to force him to break ranks and flee. A Molotov cocktail (gasoline-filled coke bottle) is a great help and, if beyond arm's throw, use an "M-16." This is what we called a special contraption we rigged up from a shotgun; it was made of a cartridge with long wooden rod substituted for projectile, and the cocktail fastened on the forward end of the rod. Using a simple bipod of two sticks, we attained surprising accuracy and effectiveness up to 100 meters. It is an ideal weapon for attacking an enemy's inflammable installations and also makes an effective antitank weapon. Once the enemy is overrun, the platoons recover their packs and resume normal activities.

Being constantly on the go creates strong bonds of both brotherhood and rivalry. Keep the rivalry healthy by explaining guerrilla social aims and personal obligations. Commanders must set examples of self-sacrifice, and they must promote bravery, ability, and personal sacrifice.

Local civilian residents are easily impressed. To stay on their good side, guerrilla leaders provide indoctrination and the troops behave themselves with care. The troops must be polite when demanding services and food and must be exhorted to keep constantly on their best behavior.

Guerrilla discipline, combat ability, and morale are put to their greatest test when the troops are encircled by the enemy. During the Cuban war, the term "siege anxiety" came into use to describe the frightened conduct of some of the troops. The deposed government arrogantly called its campaigns "siege and annihilation." Yet a well-trained, ideologically secure guerrilla force is not disturbed by this sort of campaign. Do not panic. Dig in, duck from enemy assaults, and await nightfall—your natural ally. Before darkness, pick out the best escape route. After nightfall, move out with stealth and silence. It will be exceedingly difficult for the enemy to stop you.

4. *Combat*

Combat is the climax of guerrilla life. Though each individual encounter may be only of brief duration, each battle is a profound emotional experience for the guerrilla.

Victory must be the aim of every attack. In the first stage of guerrilla warfare conducted in irregular terrain, enemy columns will make deep incursions into rebel territory. It is not difficult to ambush the leading elements and make off with their arms, ammunition, and gear while the main body is momentarily held at bay. If the guerrilla positions are strong enough, you can encircle the whole column. Be sure you have a well-dug-in force against the enemy's front, then hit him hard from the rear. If the location chosen is a natural defile, it should be easy to trap and cut to pieces an enemy force eight to ten times the size of your own. If neither of these is feasible, try the "minuet." You will not capture any supplies thereby, but with a minimum of personal risk and ammunition, you can severely weaken the enemy for a later kill.

To hit a regular convoy or position, go after an advance post at night by surprise, then exploit your success for all it's worth. Guard escape routes and ambush reinforcements.

The enemy probably has artillery, mortars, aircraft, and tanks. In irregular terrain, tanks are too road-bound to be dangerous. Mines and tank traps make the best antitank weapons, but in hand-to-hand combat, the Molotov cocktail is highly effective. (We have already mentioned the bazooka, a highly valuable weapon, but difficult to obtain in the early stages of guerrilla warfare.) Artillery or mortar fire is most effective against troops packed inside the encirclement, not those moving around outside, especially if they have fox holes to duck into. Even with high-explosive and napalm bombs, aircraft do not present a serious threat, because the guerrillas will be small, scattered targets dug in close to the enemy.

Remote-control mines are the most efficient, but their manufacture requires a degree of technical skill that is not always available. Contact mines, fuses, and electrically wired mines are highly useful and particularly difficult to breach in mountainous areas. Also, conventional tank traps are excellent for stopping mechanized forces, especially when the vehicles are buttoned up or used at night.

The enemy frequently uses open trucks preceded by

armored vehicles in his troop movements. A guerrilla force can encircle and decimate an entire column advancing in this fashion. The 16-gauge shotgun loaded with buckshot, and grenades if available, are excellent weapons for this job. After a successful attack, the guerrilla force should withdraw rapidly with captured enemy supplies.

When in defensive or blocking position, use surprise to deceive the enemy as to the location of your defensive lines and the time he will first be hit by your fire. Because they are naturally talkative and always subject to enemy terrorism, local farmers might reveal your plans to the enemy. Therefore, it is best to operate at night and to trust no one except men of proved discretion and loyalty. Carry enough food to be able to lie in wait for three or four days.

In general, the site of ambush should be at least a day's march from the permanent guerrilla encampment, the location of which is usually known to the enemy.

As stated before, the opponents can be distinguished by the character of their fires. The enemy, well supplied with ammunition, is characterized by impulsive fire in heavy volume. The guerrilla forces, not so favored, will fire sporadically—not one shot more than absolutely necessary. On the other hand, it is foolish to let the enemy escape an ambush or encirclement just to save ammunition. Decide in advance how much ammunition will have to be expended in a given situation, and enforce ammunition discipline strictly.

No guerrilla leader worthy of the name will neglect the orderly withdrawal of his forces. A withdrawal must be well timed, quick, and permit the recovery of all the wounded, of gear and ammunition. There can be no surprise attack against, or encirclement of, withdrawing forces. Therefore, the withdrawal route must be guarded in all key spots and an efficient message-relay system must be organized.

During combat, some of the troops must remain unarmed. These men, usually two to three for every ten armed soldiers, will be used to recover weapons from fallen comrades or enemy soldiers, to take charge of prisoners, to transport wounded men, or to transmit messages.

Defensive combat becomes a war of positions, yet the surprise element must be there at all times. If trenches or other defenses are built, make sure that local residents who can observe these preparations remain in your zone. As a rule, the enemy government will blockade the guerrilla region, and the local population will be forced to obtain its food and other basic supplies from distant areas. In such cases, the scorched-earth policy must be used.

Another defense tactic is to arrange things so that the enemy's leading elements always get ambushed. The pay-off is psychological: No enemy soldier will want to be in the vanguard, and a column without a vanguard cannot advance. Also, the enemy can be encircled, his flanks harassed, or his advance blocked frontally. However, be sure to secure all points where the enemy might outflank you. Offset the tendency to commit more and more men to positional defense by extensive use of tank traps and strict orders to the troops to defend their positions to death.

The more concealed an observation trench, the better. If possible, these trenches should be protected overhead against mortar fire. The mortar shells usually employed —60.1 or 85 millimeters—cannot penetrate a good, well-constructed roof made of wood, earth, and stones. Each trench must have an escape exit.

In guerrilla warfare, there is no real concept of "lines," except for moments of combat. Rather, there is a fluid no-man's land penetrated by the enemy during the day and the guerrilla at night. Through this must move guerrilla supplies, intelligence, and new recruits. Therefore, befriend the local inhabitants.

In this type of war, the work of those not directly engaged in fighting is of major importance. Communications have already been cited. Relays to headquarters or to remote guerrilla forces must be set up, utilizing the most modern means in the area. This applies to favorable as well as to unfavorable terrain.

All these examples are based on our experiences in our own war of liberation. Daily and accurate intelligence about the enemy is vital. Espionage must be well planned, and well executed by carefully chosen men. Counterespionage is a constant danger, but poor intelligence—whether exaggerating or understating—can also do great harm. Generally, men in combat will enhance and exaggerate the danger of the situation. It is not so difficult as it seems to find people to spy on the enemy: Businessmen, professionals, and even priests can be of help and give needed information.

One of the most striking characteristics of guerrilla warfare is the difference between the information available to the enemy and that available to the guerrillas. The enemy crosses hostile zones and is met by the gloomy silence of the local population. The rebel forces can generally count on friends or relatives who travel between their zone and enemy territory. But watch out should the enemy gradually advance into the zone. The male residents may flee to the guerrilla side, only to be victimized later by enemy retaliation against property and family left behind. Give them the maximum friendly support, despite the shortage of food and other difficulties certain to be encountered. Make the enemy reveal himself as the true, hated criminal.

Guerrillas seldom can spare any forces to constitute a reserve. Yet, a reserve will be needed in desperate, unforeseen situations. One way to prepare for this need is to compose an elite platoon given special privileges. Call it "The Joker" or "Suicide Platoon." Forge its reputation for heroism by committing it to the most difficult combat situations.

5. *Over-all Pattern*

Let us generalize from the Cuban experience and review the beginning, development, and end of a guerrilla war.

At first, there is a partially armed band that takes refuge in some remote, hard-to-reach spot. It strikes a lucky blow against the authorities and is joined by a few more discontented farmers, young idealists, etc. It reconnoiters inhabited areas, contacts residents, and conducts light hit-and-run attacks. As new recruits swell the band, it takes on an enemy column and destroys its leading elements. The organizational structure remains the same, but as the group grows, fewer precautionary measures are needed and it can venture into more thickly settled areas.

Next, the band sets up semipermanent encampments, establishes service echelons, and adopts the characteristics of a government in miniature. Small industries, hospitals, and radio stations are set up, laws are decreed, a court administers justice, and ideological indoctrination is intensified. An enemy attack is beaten off, more arms captured, and more guerrillas armed. When the band's radius of action no longer increases in proportion to the increase in manpower, elements are detached to form a new band operating in a new area.

The same work goes on, profiting from experience and increased guerrilla permeation of the entire region. Meanwhile, the nucleus grows with fresh support from even further areas. Officers learn new methods to develop the war and enhance their command ability through bigger responsibilities. Still more detachments strike out for new areas and the cycle begins anew.

Saboteurs infest the enemy-held open country, cutting roads and bridges, planting mines, and sowing unrest. As guerrilla warfare nears the cities, popular support rallies to the cause. Meanwhile, guerrilla combat forces capture heavier arms and begin positional warfare.

Thus, having paralyzed the enemy's logistics by sabotage and exhausted his combat forces by attrition, the guerrillas seize the initiative, attacking on all fronts at will. The enemy can stand it no longer and the remaining forces capitulate.

Given popular support and a good leader, the Cuban revolution could be duplicated in other countries. For us, Fidel Castro had the best attributes of a fighter and a statesman. His vision made possible our landing, our fight, and our triumph. This is not to say that without him victory could not have been achieved, but it would have been much more costly and less complete.

3

Organization of the Guerrilla Movement

1. Supply

SUPPLY IS THE great problem of the guerrilla. In the early stages of fighting, guerrillas must share the product of the land with the local population, for conditions will not permit the establishment of regular supply lines, lest the enemy discovers and annihilates the forces. But it will not present too difficult a problem, since natives nearly everywhere have some basic sustenance products, such as meat, salt vegetables, and grain. In eastern Cuba, it was the malanga plant; in the Mexican highland, Central America, and Peru, corn and potatoes; in Argentina, cattle; and in other regions, wheat. The local population must be won over through help and sympathy. Anyone who takes advantage of a chaotic situation and exploits the local population must be punished. In other words, all who sympathize with the revolutionary movement must be treated well; all those who attack the movement, sow dissension, or betray the guerrillas must be dealt with harshly.

As an area is taken over, the guerrillas can move about more freely. They must always pay for supplies obtained from friendly sources, whether agricultural products or manufactured goods. Often, goods and supplies will be donated, but at times the economics of a region do not permit such gifts. If lack of funds necessitates the confiscation of goods, issue IOU's. Repay all debts as soon as possible. In liberated areas, the rural population may work the fields for the guerrilla forces and guarantee them adequate, permanent sources of supplies. If necessary, the guerrillas may help the peasants work the fields. Later, they can collect all farm output for redistribution to local residents, after meeting their own needs. Taxes may be imposed to assist the guerrilla treasury. These should be as light as possible, especially for the small landholder. Good relations between the local population and the guerrillas are of paramount importance.

Taxes can be collected either in cash or in goods. Meat is a vital commodity whose production must be

53

safeguarded. Farmers should be asked to breed chickens, goats, and hogs—obtained either through purchase or confiscation. Large herds roaming uncultivated areas can be killed and their meat preserved for future use. Their hides should be tanned and used for shoes.

Supplies should be moved during the night and stored during daytime. Only those directly involved in the movement of supplies are to know the storage points. Even those living in houses used for storage should learn as little as possible about the supply lines. Mules can be used for movement. They are hardy and untiring, and a single animal can carry a load of 220 pounds. They should be well shod and driven by experienced men. Under good conditions, trucks can also be used at night.

2. *Civil Administration*

Civil administration has to be set up within and outside guerrilla territory. Despite some differences, many of the functions on both these fronts overlap.

Let us discuss guerrilla territory first. There, various administrative offices are to be organized. In Cuba, propaganda and public health (including hospitals), were under rebel-army control. Other civil functions were regulated and institutionalized by a judge advocate. These included finance, taxation, accounting, warehousing, civil law, and farmer organizations.

Do not impoverish the area and thereby feed adverse propaganda. No legal restrictions should prevent farmers from selling their produce outside the area, unless absolutely necessary. Every guerrilla action should be explained to the farm population in easily understandable language. Farmer organizations should not be limited to rebel-held territory, but extend into adjacent zones. The farmers will become disseminators of favorable propaganda, spreading tales about their life and about the spirit of sacrifice that permeates the guerrilla forces. The farmer organizations should make provisions for selling produce in enemy territory through a series of more or less friendly middlemen who will run risks for the sake of business and profit.

The importance of road construction—from narrow footpaths to good truck roads—has already been mentioned. But remember that a strong enemy can destroy roads or use them in his offensives. Therefore, as a general rule, only roads vital to the maintenance of a supply line should be built and only when you are sure that they can be defended against enemy attack. Never run unnecessary risks to build roads.

Persons familiar with the law of the land and the

needs of the area should be put in charge of the courts. In Cuba, we actually established our own penal code, civil code, regulations for supplying farmers, and agrarian-reform law.

All the above are merely recommendations—based on the experience of a certain area in a certain historical situation—that can be adapted to the needs of other areas and conditions.

Public health is a major problem. All possible assistance should be given to the local population, most of whom are totally ignorant of the most elementary principles of hygiene.

Outside guerrilla territory the functions differ. Propaganda should be of a broader educational nature, stressing guerrilla victories. Tax collections must be conducted clandestinely by province, state, city, or village finance committees. Taxes can be rendered in form of bonds or direct donations, and in the more advanced stages of war, direct taxes can be levied on industrialists. Sabotage activities are to be coordinated with the central command. Under special conditions, assassinations of individuals guilty of major repressive actions are permissible. No indiscriminate terrorism is to be employed. It is far better to try to win over large groups who can be mobilized to support the revolution when the time is ripe. Set up workers' and farmers' organizations, supply them with literature, teach them the truth. Thus the masses will be won over and their most responsible people will join in the fight.

This is the framework of civil administration inside and outside guerrilla territory. Everything here outlined can be improved. I repeat once more: Everything I have said is based on my experience in Cuba. Other conditions may call for different tactics. We are concerned with providing an outline, not a Bible.

3. *The Role of Women*

Women can play an extraordinarily important role in the development of a revolutionary process. This must be emphasized, for those of a colonial mentality tend to underestimate and discriminate against women. They are capable of the most difficult deeds, of fighting with the troops, and they do not cause sexual conflicts among the troops, as has been charged. Women, although weaker than men, are no less resilient. They can fight, and they have played an outstanding role in the Cuban war.

Of course, there are not too many women soldiers. But they can be used in many capacities, particularly in communications. They should be entrusted with carrying confidential messages, ammunition, etc. If captured, they will invariably be treated better than men, no matter how brutal the enemy. They can cook for the troops and perform other duties of a domestic nature, teach the soldiers and the local population, indoctrinate the children, perform the functions of social workers, nurse the sick, help sew uniforms, and, if necessary, even bear arms. In Cuba, many successful marriages were contracted within the guerrilla forces.

4. Medical Care

The doctor's role in guerrilla life is a highly important one. Not only does he save lives, but he strengthens the morale of the sick and wounded. Guerrilla medical care ranges from the simple front-line doctor, often bearing arms, to the doctor enjoying staff and hospital facilities. In all phases, he must possess a keen appreciation of revolutionary aims. Proper moral support is often a vital part of successful treatment. An ordinary aspirin administered by a sympathetic, understanding man can mean a great deal to a suffering soldier. In the "seminomad" phase of guerrilla warfare, temporary medical stations where emergency surgery can be performed can be set up in friendly households. In the advance phase, regular hospitals equipped with laboratories, diagnostic facilities, and X-ray equipment can be established.

Sometimes medicines can be obtained from health organizations, including the Red Cross, but don't count on this, especially at the beginning. Various types of doctors are needed: general practitioners, anesthetists, surgeons, orthopedists, and dentists.

5. Sabotage

Sabotage is one of the invaluable weapons of guerrilla warfare. It is to be conducted outside rebel-held territory and directed by the guerrilla general staff. Sabotage is not terrorism. On a national scale, its aim is the interruption of enemy communications—telephone and telegraph installations, bridges, railroads. Vital industries and businesses owned by enemy leaders also may have to be destroyed, but indiscriminate destruction resulting in mass starvation and unemployment is impermissible.

In combat-zone sabotage, strike boldly and frequently, using guerrilla flying squads to support civilian action. Again, the emphasis is on interrupting communications. Also, knock out enemy supply sources.

Give the enemy no rest. Constant nagging and harassment will dissipate much valuable enemy strength.

6. *Guerrilla Industry*

Guerrilla industry is the product of a fairly long development. Set up industries as soon as taking control of an area. The two most vital industries are shoe and harness making. Shoes are essential and can be manufactured in small shops manned by the local population. Other essential products include cartridge belts, canvas and leather packs, improvised weapons, explosives, fuses, grenades, canteens, cigars and cigarettes, and leather.

7. *Propaganda*

The ideas governing the revolution should be disseminated in depth. The propaganda effort should be well organized and carried out by two staffs: one for the nation as a whole, the other for the guerrilla forces. Both of these should be coordinated by one director.

Spread national propaganda via periodicals, newspapers, radio, and special leaflets for farmers, workers, and enemy soldiers. Tell the truth about the guerrilla situation, explain aims, announce aid received, discuss necessary sabotage, proclaim slogans, denounce enemy crimes and criminals, etc.

The most effective propaganda is carried on within the guerrilla zone. Supplement radio broadcasts and printed information with word-of-mouth instructions about air-raid defenses, enemy locations, etc. Information for foreign news sources should confine itself to facts about the war.

Radio is the most effective propaganda channel, able to disseminate impassioned appeals all over the country. It can explain, educate, and influence. Stick to the truth. Remember, a small truth well presented is far better than the most glittering lie. Broadcast fresh news of all battles, enemy terror, guerrilla doctrine, how-to-do-it instruction, and speeches by guerrilla leaders.

8. *Intelligence*

"Know yourself and your enemy and you will be able to win a hundred battles." Nothing helps the combat forces more than accurate intelligence. You can expect the local residents to be a spontaneous source of information. But be sure to sort fact from fiction. As soon as post offices and mail deliveries can be set up within the guerrilla zone, try to get intelligence about the enemy. Use women to infiltrate the enemy camp. Use trained men and women to spread rumors and sow confusion and fear among the enemy.

9. Indoctrination and Training

In the beginning, the guerrilla soldier learns his craft on his own, through the very life he lives, and there is no such thing as a guerrilla leader who has not gone through this daily self-training. A comrade may teach a soldier a little about the use of arms, combat tactics, how to deal with civilians, etc., but the precious time of the guerrilla should not be wasted on regular training courses. Later, after a sizable area has been liberated, recruit schools can be set up. These schools will train new soldiers who have not experienced the hardships of the early guerrilla forces. Recruits get their own supplies and do their own housekeeping. They are toughened by commando courses and long, arduous marches. The recruit centers have their own medical services. Stress rifle marksmanship and ammunition discipline. If enough ammunition is available, let the recruits practice with live ammunition.

Our Cuban school was spotted by the enemy, and we were subjected to real aerial attacks twice daily.

The way in which the trainee reacted to these attacks told something about his combat potential.

Since recruits join up with fuzzy concepts of liberty, freedom of the press, etc., they need indoctrination on guerrilla aims, economic factors and motivations of national history, national heroes, behavior in face of injustice, analysis of the current situation. Set up teacher-training centers and prepare textbooks for indoctrination. Encourage reading and supervise the choice of books. Above all, inculcate a reasoning, not a mechanical, self-discipline. This is the best assurance for success when the chips are down in combat. Gradually, standards are raised in the school and hence throughout the whole guerrilla force.

10. Over-all Leadership

Any guerrilla revolutionary army must have a structured, over-all leadership. In Cuba, we had a commander in chief who appointed regional chiefs. They, in turn, appointed majors in charge of columns and other, lower-ranking officers.

This set-up is not necessarily a model to be followed. It is merely the description of how we organized an effective, victorious army. In the last analysis, rank itself is of little importance. What matters is that no rank should be conferred on anyone who has not stood the test of battle.

The organizational structure here described is intended for an army ready to go into combat, not for the initial stages of guerrilla warfare, in which a leader may assume a high rank if he so chooses, but commands only a small group of men.

Discipline is necessary. It must be based on reason and personal conviction. Breach of discipline must be punished drastically and painfully. A guardhouse sentence may merely seem like a much-desired rest to a soldier, a period in which he can eat to his heart's content, without marches, work, or guard duty, with plenty of sleep and leisure time. Therefore, deprivation of liberty does not have the desired results and is not recommended. But deprivation of the right to carry arms will work in the case of a highly motivated individual. For example, we caught a soldier snoozing in an easy chair when he should have been on duty. We took his rifle away and told him to win the right to another one in combat. A few days later, we found him dying in a hospital after a battle. He told us with pride how he had won his right to bear arms again. This is the type of morale that we were able to achieve in our troops.

Long guard duty and forced marches can also be

used as punishment. But marches only tire the soldier and the guards accompanying him. And soldiers assigned to punitive guard duty also have to be watched by other guards.

In the forces directly under my command, I introduced arrest with deprivation of candy and cigarettes (for light offenders), and total deprivation of food (for serious offenders). The results were wonderful, but the punishment was very drastic and is advisable only under very special circumstances.

4

Appendix

1. The Organization of the Initial Clandestine Guerrilla Band

GUERRILLA WARFARE IS governed by general laws of warfare, but since it starts with a conspiracy, it is also governed by laws uniquely its own. If there exists a spontaneous, popular feeling against coercion, it may be possible to organize guerrilla warfare on the spot. But, in general, the struggle is begun abroad or in an isolated spot, centered around some respected leader fighting for the salvation of his people.

Almost all recent popular movements have suffered from inadequate preparation. Frequently, the secret service of the governing rulers learns about planned conspiracies. Absolute secrecy is crucial. The human material must be chosen with care. At times, this selection is easy; at others, extremely difficult. One has to make do with those who are available—exiles and volunteers eager to join in the fight for liberation. There is no adequate investigative apparatus. Yet there is no excuse for intelligence reaching the enemy, even if the guerrilla organization has been infiltrated by spies, for no more than one or two persons should be familiar with preparatory plans. Keep new volunteers away from key places.

Absolutely nobody must learn anything beyond his immediate concern. Never discuss plans with anyone. Check incoming and outgoing mail. Know what contacts each member has. Work and live in teams, never individually. Trust no one beyond the nucleus, especially not women. The enemy will undoubtedly try to use women for espionage. The revolutionary secretly preparing for war must be an ascetic and perfectly disciplined. Anyone who repeatedly defies the orders of his superiors and makes contact with women and other outsiders, however innocuous, must be expelled immediately for violation of revolutionary discipline.

Given suitable operating terrain, land hunger, enemy injustices, etc., a hard core of thirty to fifty men is, in my opinion, enough to initiate armed revolution in any Latin American country.

As has been stated before, arms should be of the type used by the enemy. In most cases, individual units should not comprise more than fifty to one hundred men. Of course, there is no reason why you cannot have a nucleus of 500 men, but these 500 must be split up, because (a) so large a group is bound to attract attention, and (b) in case of betrayal, the entire force could be liquidated.

The location of headquarters may be revealed to most of the group and serve as the meeting place for the volunteers, but the leaders of the conspiracy should appear there only rarely and no compromising documents are to be kept there. The leaders should stay in dispersed, secret hiding places. Locations of arsenals should not be known to more than one or two persons. Arms are not to be distributed until the operation is ready to start, so as not to endanger those involved and to avoid possible loss of costly equipment.

The struggle will be hard, long, and will meet with reverses; only high morale, strict discipline, and deep faith in ultimate victory will sustain the forces. In Cuba, a nucleus of twelve dedicated men—plus a Fidel Castro—were able to succeed.

Physical and ideological training — exhausting marches, target practice, map-reading courses—must prepare the men for the extreme hardships certain to be encountered before victory is achieved.

2. Defending That Which Has Been Won

Final liberation comes only with the total systematic break-up of the enemy army and all institutions that supported the old regime. At this point world public opinion, the "responsible press," the "truthful" news agencies of the United States and other monopolistic countries will be sure to attack the liberated country. Therefore, no trace of the old army and its soldiers can remain. Militarism, blind obedience, old concepts of military duty, discipline, and morale cannot be uprooted as long as the victors—noble, good, but generally uneducated—tolerate the defeated—well-trained, knowledgeable in the war sciences, full of hatred against the guerrillas.

Revolutionary action must be rededicated by forging a new army with technical skill, unshakable ideology, and great combat power. At this stage, begin to prepare for the new defensive war the people's army may have to fight. In the wake of victory, thousands of belated revolutionaries will want to join. These will have to undergo guerrilla-warfare training and indoctrination. Set up a propaganda organization to disseminate the new truths about the revolution among army units. Carry the campaign to the soldiers, the rural population, the workers; tell them of the goals of the revolution, explain why they fought, why their comrades died. Educate them; wipe out illiteracy. Forge the new army into a highly skilled force with a solid ideology and great combat power. All this will take time. Once the best survivors of the enemy army have been trained ideologically, use them to improve professional and technical standards.

Everything that follows is the opinion of the leaders of the rebel army with regard to Cuban policy. The leaders have fearlessly analyzed and evaluated the concrete threat of a foreign invasion, which they expect at the end of 1959 or early 1960. We will not theorize about what is already known to all, but we will draw inferences from existing facts in order to strengthen our national defense. We herewith present our analysis as an epilogue.

3. Epilogue. An Analysis of the Cuban Situation: Its Present and Its Future

A year has passed since the dictator has been put to flight after a long struggle. Our government has been

able to chalk up enormous social, economic, and political gains. Our national revolution, basically agrarian
but enjoying the enthusiastic support of workers, the
middle class, and even industrialists, has acquired international significance. It is supported by the will of the
people. This epilogue is not meant as a synthesis of all
the laws promulgated. Let us just emphasize the significance of some of them as respects the state's attention
to the needs of the Cuban people. First came the rent
laws and the reduction of public-utility rates. Soon the
parasites who at first thought Fidel Castro and the
other men who made this revolution, these malleable,
stupid, bearded men, were just another version of old-
style politicians, began to suspect that something more
profound was emerging, that their prerogatives were in
danger of disappearing. The word "Communism" began to be bruited about in connection with the victorious guerrillas, and "anti-Communism" became the
rallying cry of those dispossessed of their ill-gotten gains.

Tenant-farming and installment-buying regulations
also contributed to the feeling of unease. But these
were little skirmishes. They still hoped that "that
lunatic" Fidel Castro could be advised and steered onto
good, "democratic" paths by a Dubois or a Porter.
They hoped for the future.

The agrarian-reform law came as a tremendous blow.
Their eyes were opened. Gaston Baquero, the spokes-

man of reaction, fled to the more tranquil waters of dictatorial Spain. Others still felt that "the law is the law," and that other governments had also passed laws theoretically meant to benefit all the people. But the implementation of the laws was another thing. INRA (National Institute for Agrarian Reform), that mischievous and complicated child, was looked at with amused tolerance by respectable social scientists and economists living in a world far removed from the uneducated, childish guerrillas. But INRA rolled on like a tank, breaking the large landholdings and instituting new social conditions of land ownership. The Cuban Agrarian Reform was antifeudal insofar as it abolished all vestiges of tenant farming and servitude in the coffee and tobacco plantations. It enabled the farmers individually or collectively to work their land without fear of creditor or owner. It assured peasants and agricultural workers of technical advice, financial assistance, and machinery, and it organized farmers' cooperatives. These state warehouses, paying a fair price for the harvests, are in the process of displacing the old "bloodsuckers."

In forging ahead with our Agrarian Reform Law, we have done a more thorough and quicker job than ever was done in the other three Latin American countries that instituted such programs—Mexico, Guatemala, and Bolivia. Our agrarian reform respects only the right of the people. It does not seek to revenge itself against any class or nationality. The law applies to the United Fruit Company or the King Ranch just as it does to Cuban landowners.

Under these conditions, rice, seed, and cotton production is developing rapidly. But we are not satisfied with these accomplishments. We will win back all our stolen wealth. The petroleum law has restored our subsoil to us. It meets the overwhelming needs of a people who want to be free, who want to be masters of their economy, who want to prosper and develop. The example we are setting has instilled fear into the oil monopolies. Not that Cuba can inflict great harm on them; we are not a major source of this valuable fuel, although we hope to produce enough oil to meet domestic requirements. But our example demonstrates to other Latin American countries, many of whom are controlled by the monopolists and some of whom have been driven into civil wars to propitiate the needs of the giant trusts, what can be done and when it should be done. The big monopolies also are worried by Cuba. Not only because our small Caribbean island has dared liquidate the omnipotent legacy left by John Foster Dulles to his heirs—the United Fruit Company—but also because we have dealt a blow at the Rockefeller empire and because the Deutch group interests have been seized by the Cuban people's revolution.

This law, like that on mining, is the people's answer to those who threaten them with force, aerial attacks, and other punitive measures. In the opinion of some, the mining law is as important as agrarian reform. We do not quite share this opinion, but the 25-per-cent export tax levied against companies exporting primary products not only will contribute to the well-being of Cuba, but also increase the relative power of the Canadian monopolies in their fight with the present exploiters of nickel ore. Thus the Cuban revolution, by liquidating large landholdings, is also limiting foreign monopoly and import profits. In launching a new policy in the Americas, it has also attempted to break the monopoly of the giant mining companies, creating problems for at least one of them. Not only is this policy a clarion call to all Latin American neighbors, but it has had repercussions all over the Americas. The Cuban revolution is breaking all news barriers and disseminating the truth among all Latin American masses yearning for a better life. Cuba is the symbol of a new concept of nationalism, and Fidel Castro the symbol of liberation.

This little 114,000-square-kilometer island, inhabited by 6.5 million people, has become the leader of the anticolonial struggle in the Americas. Those American countries who, stronger than we, are trying to develop a national capitalism in the face of foreign monopolies, are becoming aware of this new, small force for liberty, for their governments lack sufficient resources to see the fight through to the bitter end. It is not an easy fight, nor is it devoid of danger or difficulty. Isolated as we are in the Americas, it requires the support of all the people, idealism, and a spirit of sacrifice. In the past, small countries tried to do the job. Guatemala— the Guatemala of the quetzal bird, which dies when imprisoned, the Guatemala of Tecum Uman—became a victim of direct colonialist aggression. And Bolivia —the country of Morillo, the protomartyr of American independence—succumbed in the terrible struggle, after having given the Cuban revolution three outstanding examples: the abolition of the army, agrarian reform, and the nationalization of its mines, the major source of Bolivia's wealth and its greatest source of tragedy.

Cuba is aware of these examples and of the errors and difficulties it faces. But it also knows that a new world is dawning. The pillars of colonialism are crumbling in the face of national and popular struggles in Asia and Africa. The people are united, not by religion, race, custom, or hunger, but by common economic and social goals and by a common desire to improve their lot. Asia and Africa joined in Bandung. Now Cuba is uniting Asia and Africa with colonial America.

The great colonial powers are capitulating to the peoples' demands. Belgium and Holland are merely caricatures of empires. Germany and Italy have lost their colonies. France is replotting her course after a bitter war. England, diplomatic and prudent, is liquidating her political power but maintaining her economic ties.

U.S. capitalism has replaced some of the traditional colonialism until recently in power in the newly independent countries, but this is a passing phase. The U.S.A. has not really established its financial power in the new territories. The claws of the American eagle have been filed down. Colonialism has perished, or is about to perish, in many areas of the world.

The Americas are another matter. Some time ago, the British lion let go of our part of the Americas, and the young Yankee capitalists established a "democratic" version of British club life, imposing their sovereign domination in each of the twenty Latin American republics.

This is the colonial satrapy of U.S. monopoly, its "backyard," its reason and only hope for existence. If all Latin American peoples raised the banner of dignity, as Cuba has done, the monopolists would tremble and accommodate themselves to a new politicoeconomic situation. Monopolies do not like to cut their profits, and the Cuban example—this "bad example"—is winning ground in other Latin American countries. Each time an oppressed people cries out for liberation, Cuba is blamed. It is blamed because in a sense it is guilty of having shown how an armed popular force can defeat supposedly invincible armies, how the enemy can be worn down and destroyed in rugged mountain terrain.

Cuba has set a very bad example. Monopolies cannot rest easy while this bad example continues to exist, to face up to danger, to advance toward the future. Their spokesmen proclaim that we must be destroyed. It is necessary, so say the lackeys of monopoly disguised as congressmen, to intervene in this "bastion of Communism." "The Cuban situation is causing us much concern," say the defenders of trusts. What they really mean is: It is necessary to destroy Cuba.

Well, what are their prospects of success? First there is the purely economic weapon. The U.S.A. can restrict bank credits and stop suppliers from servicing our merchants and banks. It could induce Western Europe to do likewise. But this alone would not be enough.

Initially, credit restrictions would make great inroads on our economy, but they would boomerang, and the victimized country would adjust itself to a day-to-day existence. Pressures would have to be applied. The sugar quota would enter the picture: Yes, no, no, yes. The monopolists would begin to calculate all the risks and arrive at the conclusion that it would be very dangerous to lower the Cuban quota, and impossible to abolish it.

Why dangerous? Because, quite aside from the fact that it would be inadvisable, the ten or fifteen sugar-supplying countries greedily would demand more than they are now receiving. It would be impossible, because Cuba is the biggest, cheapest source of sugar for the U.S.A., and because 60 per cent of the production and marketing facilities belong to the U.S.A. Moreover, the trade balance is favorable to the United States. He who does not sell cannot buy, and breaking a treaty would set a bad example. But that is not the point. The so-called U.S. gift of paying about 3 cents more than the market price is based on their inability to produce cheap sugar. High wages and low productivity prevent U.S.A. sugar production from meeting Cuban prices. Protected by the higher price they pay for a product, they impose onerous treaties on all the beneficiaries, not only on Cuba. It would be impossible to liquidate the Cuban quota.

We do not pay serious attention to a possible bombardment and burning of cane fields. This threat seems to be intended merely as an attempt to weaken the revolutionary government in the eyes of the population.

The Cuban economy is vulnerable in other areas also, for example, the supply of raw materials such as cotton. But since the world suffers from an overproduction of cotton, this problem is of a transitory nature. Fuel is an important item. Lack of fuel can paralyze a country, and Cuba produces very little. It has some tars and some industrial alcohol. But there is much oil in the world. Egypt and the Soviet Union can sell us some, and perhaps Iraq will be able to sell some in the near future.

In addition to economic pressures, there exists the possibility of interference by a "pocket power," such as the Dominican Republic, for example. Such aggression would cause some problems, but in the end the United Nations would have to intervene. Incidentally, the new policy of the Organization of American States sets a dangerous precedent in the case of intervention. Hiding behind Trujillo, the monopolies continue to build their structure of aggression. It is sad that Venezuela has placed us in the difficult position of having to refuse to intervene against Trujillo.

Of course, there is always the possibility of killing that "lunatic" Fidel Castro, the target of monopolistic wrath. Naturally, it would also be necessary to eliminate those two other dangerous "international agents," Raul Castro and the writer of this article. It is a tempting prospect. (However, gentlemen of the monopolies, don't forget the people. They would destroy and wreak vengeance on all those who may, directly or indirectly, be connected with the assassination of the leaders of the revolution. Nothing and nobody could stop them.)

Another aspect of the Guatemalan variant is to choke

79

off Cuba's arms supply, forcing her to obtain them from Communist countries, and then to unleash a violent tirade against her for doing so. But a member of our government has summed this up as follows: "They may attack us for being 'Communists,' but they are not going to wipe us out merely because we were stupid." Finally, the monopolists may consider direct aggression necessary and are probably trying to figure out the prospects on their IBM machines. They may use the Spanish tactics; i.e., exiles and volunteers—mercenaries or foreign soldiers supported by air and naval forces. Or perhaps we would be attacked directly by another country, such as the Dominican Republic, which would send its soldiers—our brothers—to die on our beaches and provoke an act of war. This would compel the clever strongholds of the monopolies to declare that they do not wish to intervene in this "disastrous" internecine war. They would use battleships, cruisers, destroyers, aircraft carriers, submarines, minesweepers, torpedo boats, and aircraft to guard the sea and the sky to prevent supplies from flowing to Cuba, but Trujillo's forces would succeed in eluding their watchful eye. Also, they could intervene through some prestige-laden inter-American organization, demanding an end to the "terrible war" that "Communism" has unleashed on our island, or, should this fail, they could intervene directly, protesting that they are acting to maintain peace and protect the interests of the Cuban people—à la Korea.

But perhaps the first aggressive act would not be directed against us, but rather against the legal government of Venezuela, wiping out the last friendly power in Latin America. Should this happen, Bolivar's fatherland rather than Cuba may very well become the stage on which the battle against colonialism will be fought. The people of Venezuela, aware that defeat would spell tyranny, would defend their freedom, would defend liberty with all their might, in the knowledge that a series of successful people's wars may help destroy the monopolistic cemeteries into which our subjugated sister countries have been converted.

There are many reasons why the enemy cannot be victorious. This is 1960, the year of the underdeveloped countries, the year of the liberated peoples, the year in which the voice of those millions not governed by the merchants of death will be heard. Furthermore—and still more convincing—6 million Cubans will rise as one man to defend their land and their revolution. A nation in arms under dynamic leadership, ideologically secure, will fight its battle in every part of the country. The workers in the cities will die in defense of their factories; the farmers will kill the invaders from behind the new mechanical plows the revolution has given them.

And throughout the world, millions of people will rise up to protest aggression. The monopolies will witness the destruction of their pillars. But suppose they dare oppose world opinion. What would happen then? We, on our vulnerable island, without heavy arms, would fight a guerrilla war. Our units would fight with all the fervor, conviction, and enthusiasm of which the sons of the Cuban revolution are capable in this glorious year of our history. In other words, should the enemy destroy our forces we are ready to transform ourselves into a guerrilla army, a mobile force under good leadership and a central command able to coordinate strategy.

The mountains would be the last defense line of the vanguard rebel army. But the struggle would be carried on in every house, every street, every hill, every inch of our territory by our rear guard—our trained and armed population.

Since our infantry does not own heavy equipment, they would concentrate on antitank and anti-aircraft defense. Mines, bazookas, grenades, anti-aircraft guns, and mortars would be our arms. The veteran infantry soldier in possession of automatic weapons would know the value of ammunition. Our air force would probably sustain heavy damage in the early stages of an invasion by a major foreign power. It would be crippled or perhaps destroyed. We would be left only with reconnaissance planes and helicopters.

The navy would use small launches of maximum mobility. The enemy army would not find any solid object to attack. Everything would be an amorphous mass—moving, impenetrable, striking blows, and not offering a solid front.

A people's army of farmers and workers eager to defend its country cannot be easily defeated, even though sustaining heavy blows. The farmers near Pinar del Rio have already shown that they are able to defeat small gangs. The farmers will be trained by us on their territory. But their officers will be, and are being, trained at our military bases. From these bases, they will go forth into the thirty agrarian zones into which our country has been divided, forming thirty centers of resistance to defend their land, their achievements, their new homes, their canals, their dikes, their harvest, their independence, their right to life.

They will oppose any enemy advance and, if overpowered, they will split up and return to the land, tilling the soil during the day, fighting the enemy at night. The workers will act in a similar fashion. The best of them will be trained for leadership and defense. Every social group will have its own function. The peasant will carry on guerrilla warfare, learning to shoot, to take advantage of the terrain. The worker will learn to erect barricades on the streets, to use houses and factories as fortresses, to hurl Molotov cocktails, to shoot from houses. Thus a powerful army will be forged from the masses of workers, the police, and the army. Urban fighting will not be as elastic as guerrilla warfare in the countryside. Many of us will die in this war.

There will be organizations other than those of the workers and peasants. A student militia, led and coordinated by the rebel army, will contain the cream of student youth. Other youth and women's organizations will also participate in the struggle. The women will assist their comrades by cooking, nursing the wounded, comforting the dying, instilling confidence in the fighters. All this will be accomplished. And beyond this, the masses will be educated and told the facts about the revolution.

Revolutionary law must be discussed, explained, and studied in every meeting, every gathering, every assembly of people. The speeches of the leaders must be read and discussed—especially those of Fidel Castro. They must be broadcast by radio and television to all corners of the country.

The people must know every law, decree, and resolution. Revolutionary vigilance must be exercised over every oppositional act, over morals, over antirevolutionaries, over the disaffected. No breach of morals, even if committed by a deserving revolutionary, can go unpunished. Previous service to the cause may be considered an extenuating factor but not an excuse. Collective work must be emphasized. Encourage the voluntary construction of roads, bridges, piers, and student centers.

Any army so welded to the people—the peasants and workers from whom it sprang—an army so conversant with strategy and ideologically secure, such an army is invincible. For that and all the other reasons, and in spite of the monopolists' understandable wish to destroy the "bad example" of Cuba, our future is brighter than ever.